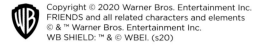
Running Press
Hachette Book Group
1290 Avenue of the Americas, New York, NY 10104
www.runningpress.com
@Running_Press

Printed in China

First Edition: October 2020

Published by Running Press, an imprint of Perseus Books, LLC, a subsidiary of Hachette Book Group, Inc. The Running Press name and logo is a trademark of the Hachette Book Group.

The Hachette Speakers Bureau provides a wide range of authors for speaking events. To find out more, go to www.hachettespeakersbureau.com or call (866) 376-6591.

The publisher is not responsible for websites (or their content) that are not owned by the publisher.

Image credits can be found on page 176.

Print book interior design by Tandem Books.

Library of Congress Control Number: 2020936610

ISBNs: 978-0-7624-9930-4 (hardcover), 978-0-7624-9931-1 (ebook)

1010

10 9 8 7 6 5 4 3 2 1

F·R·I·E·N·D·S
THE TELEVISION SERIES

FRIENDSGIVING

THE OFFICIAL GUIDE TO HOSTING, ROASTING, AND CELEBRATING WITH FRIENDS

SHOSHANA STOPEK

Running Press
PHILADELPHIA

CONTENTS

Part Two
ENTERTAINING
77

Part Three
ACTIVITIES
133

FRIENDS AND FRIENDSGIVING:
MEANT TO BE TOGETHER

STRANGELY ENOUGH, YOU WON'T hear the term "Friendsgiving" in any episode of *Friends*. In fact, the phrase didn't come about until 2007, three years after the show's ten-year run (1994–2004) ended. Still, there's no denying that *Friends* had a major influence on this friends-first holiday. Many articles have been written about how more and more people host a dinner just for their friends to mark the holiday in addition to having a traditional Thanksgiving feast with their families. But *Friends* Thanksgivings were about being with the people who mattered most.

From the famous football game to the "I Hate Rachel Green" Club to meat sweats, a dancing turkey, righteous mac 'n' cheese, and a severed toe, *Friends* Thanksgiving episodes brought us some iconic moments. And, let's face it, no one knows how to work a party and a pair of Thanksgiving pants better than *Friends*. But beneath the humor, we also found meaning as we watched six friends year after year give themselves permission to celebrate Thanksgiving with each other instead of with their families.

Friendsgiving Is about Gratitude

In true Chandler form, Chandler offers this cynical toast to the gang to commemorate their first Thanksgiving together in "The One Where Underdog Gets Away." It's a moment that acknowledges the love-hate relationship many of us have with the age-old traditions associated with the holiday, but

"So I guess what I'm trying to say is that I'm very thankful that all of your Thanksgivings sucked."

—Chandler Bing, "The One Where Underdog Gets Away"

Monica tells the gang "This Thanksgiving kicks last Thanksgiving's ass" after learning that she and Chandler have been chosen as adoptive parents ("The One With the Late Thanksgiving").

more importantly, it's a moment when we see the gang come together and form a new kind of family and a new tradition.

Friendsgiving Is Perfectly Imperfect

Remember that to get to the moment of Chandler's toast, everyone's plans (except Phoebe's, which were apparently nonexistent) had to fall apart. Ross and Monica's parents go out of town, Rachel can't afford a flight, Joey's family uninvites him after seeing his ad for VD, and Chandler boycotts all "pilgrim holidays" due to childhood trauma. Even the Thanksgiving Underdog float can't get it together, as it sadly makes a break for it during the parade. The meal is hardly what one might call

Eating Rachel's trifle doesn't come easily to anyone, except Joey:

"What's not to like? Custard: good! Jam: good! Meat: goooood!"
—Joey Tribbiani, "The One Where Ross Got High"

perfect—grilled cheese, wine, and Funyuns take the place of a burnt turkey. But the gathering sets the stage for what will be the first of ten perfectly imperfect Thanksgivings (a.k.a. Friendsgivings) among good friends on the show.

Friendsgiving Is about Forgiveness and Togetherness

With each episode, we experience all the relatable highs and lows that many of us associate with the turkey-filled day—sibling rivalry, competitive football, reliving memories, and food at its best and worst. Whether that means fighting over who gets your baby, duking it out for the Geller Cup, finding out your friend was in a club about hating you, screwing up the trifle, getting your head stuck in a turkey, or being trapped in a box . . . ultimately, it's about forgiveness. And, at the end of the day, as Rachel points out to her sister, who shows up, uninvited, it's also about togetherness:

"It's Thanksgiving, and we should not want to be together, together."
—Rachel Green "The One With the Late Thanksgiving"

Let's Face It, Friendsgiving Is about Turkey

Joey is always there to remind us where food goes, lest we might forget. And sometimes it does get a little confusing. Whether the turkey is stuck on Joey's head, dancing and wearing sunglasses for Chandler, or devoured in one sitting, the turkey just may be the most underrated character on the show.

"Don't you put words in people's mouths. You put turkey in people's mouths."

—Joey Tribbiani, "The One With the Late Thanksgiving"

Friendsgiving Is about Friendship

At the heart of every *Friends* episode is friendship. We see the gang go through just about every imaginable experience in life together—weddings, divorces, children, job changes, family drama, and all kinds of

It's a real act of love to voluntarily put a turkey on your head ("The One With All the Thanksgivings").

day-to-day shenanigans. As they search for love, happiness, and success in their careers, it's the friendships they have with one another that are constant—just like the table that's always there for them at Central Perk. For this crew, *it's your friends who are your family*. It's this connection to the characters that we feel when we watch the show, and it's the thread that takes us back to our own lives. It's the reason why we laugh when Joey gets a turkey stuck on his head, why we cringe when Rachel discovers Ross's pros and cons list about her, and why we rejoice when we learn Monica and Chandler are getting a baby. As Monica says in that pivotal moment: "This Thanksgiving kicks last Thanksgiving's ass!" And we are right there with her, cheering her on.

So, whether you've had a string of sunny days or "when it hasn't been your day, your week, your month, or even your year," maybe it's time to get your best buds together for Friendsgiving and remind yourselves what true friends are for.

Nothing says Thanksgiving like a competitive game of touch football between siblings.

"Let go! I'm a tiny little woman."
—Monica Geller,
"The One With the Football"

The gang relives their worst Thanksgiving memories, including their 1987 turkey dinner at the Gellers ("The One With All the Thanksgivings").

Some people host Friendsgiving before Thanksgiving, while others host on the day itself, but the fact is, there are no rules. You can actually host Friendsgiving anytime you want! Whether you're a first-time host or a pro, it's easy to get overwhelmed while planning the perfect get-together. It helps to keep in mind that the point of Friendsgiving is to be with your closest friends in a joyful and stress-free way. That's why you won't find anything complicated in this book. What you will find are easy, delicious recipes, entertaining tips, and fun activities—all inspired by memorable moments from the show. So, fire up an episode, invite over your besties, and let loose with this complete guide to hosting Friendsgiving in the spirit of *Friends*.

♥ ♡ ♥ ♡ ♥ ♡ ♥ ♡ ♥ ♡ ♥

The gang gathers around the table for a Thanksgiving meal in "The One With the Late Thanksgiving."

MONICA: Hey, what are you doing? You gotta save room. You've got almost an entire turkey to eat.

JOEY: Let me explain to you how the human body works. I have to warm up my stomach first. Eating chips is like stretching. Don't worry, Tribbianis never get full.

PART ONE
RECIPES

ONE OF THE greatest joys of Friendsgiving is sharing an intimate potluck feast with your closest friends. The beauty of cooking for Friendsgiving is that you can make the menu whatever you want it to be. Whether you have a friend who is anti-Thanksgiving like Chandler, vegetarian like Phoebe, a foodie like Monica, an eater like Joey, nostalgic like Ross, or a bad cook like Rachel, you can successfully host an event that will please everyone. All you need is a little creativity, some variety (think foods that the Pilgrims *didn't* eat, for friends like Chandler), and coordination with your besties. We've got you covered from warm-up to dessert, and we promise you won't be serving a trifle that includes beef sautéed with peas and onions or a cheesecake off the floor. But you just might have your friends begging for seconds of all your treats. So get ready to slay in the kitchen like Monica would!

THE ONE WITH THE WARM-UP

THE "WARM-UP" may more commonly be known as pre-game, cocktail hour, or appetizers. What's important is that it gives your guests time to arrive and get comfortable, and it allows you time to greet everyone, finish up any loose ends, and heat anything that needs reheating.

THE TRIBBIANI CHEESE BOARD WARM-UP

Inspired by: "The One With the Rumor"

The cheese board is a classic appetizer and crowd-pleaser. The key is to have a balance of salty and sweet flavors and hard and soft cheeses. Add something crunchy and something savory for extra yumminess.

The Cheeses

A good rule of thumb is to offer three different kinds of cheeses, each one ideally served in a block or wedge (the exception is if it's spreadable):

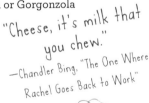

One creamy: Brie or a spreadable cheese

One hard or aged: Manchego or aged cheddar

One mild, medium-soft, or stinky cheese: Gouda or Gorgonzola

Make sure to serve each cheese with its own knife.

"Cheese, it's milk that you chew."
—Chandler Bing, "The One Where Rachel Goes Back to Work"

The Crunchy

Freshly cut slices of baguette

Some crackers or chips, in the spirit of Joey Tribbiani

An assortment of nuts such as almonds, walnuts, and pistachios (kept separate in case any of your guests have nut allergies)

"Remember when you were a kid and your mom would drop you off at the movies with a jar of jam and a little spoon?"
—Joey Tribbiani, "The One With the Jam"

The Sweet

A nice jam such as seeded raspberry, strawberry preserves, or fig

Some grapes or apple slices

Dried fruit such as apricots, cranberries, or apples

The Savory, Salty, and Sour

Some charcuterie (cured meats): prosciutto, salami, soppressata, chorizo, or mortadella

Kalamata olives

Mini gherkins

WHAT TO SERVE FOR DRINKS

Remember when Rachel and Ross had a few too many and got married in Vegas? Or when Monica announced to her parents that she was drunk at her thirtieth birthday party? That's not what you're going for here.

So what should you serve to drink at your *Friends*-themed Friendsgiving?

There are two routes you could take that would be totally *Friends* appropriate:

- Wine and beer
- A big-batch cocktail served in a punch bowl or pitcher

Whichever way you decide to go, make sure to always have some nonalcoholic options too, such as flavored sparkling waters, sodas, and flat water.

Wine and Beer

Rationale: The gang drinks wine at just about every major occasion and party. The rule of thumb is often estimated at one bottle of wine for every two people. Yes, that might sound like a lot, but one bottle serves about four large glasses and when you factor in warm-up time, dinnertime, and post-dinner activities over a period of a few hours, it makes a whole lot of sense. Understandably, you might not want to purchase such a hefty lot of alcohol, so during your planning phase, you can always ask your guests to bring one dish and one bottle. It's also a good idea to have some red and some white, some dry and some sweet, to satisfy all the most common palates.

"Hello, Vegas? Yeah, we would like some more alcohol, and you know what else? We would like some more beers."
—Rachel Green, "The One in Vegas—Part 1"

For beer, it's best to stick with classic lagers and ales and nothing too heavy. If you can find out beforehand which guests will drink wine and which will drink beer, it will help in determining quantities.

Big-Batch Cocktails

Instead of serving individual drinks, why not make one jumbo punch bowl or pitcher of something special. Both of the following recipes can be prepared with or without alcohol and are a surefire way to win over your crowd.

* * * * * * * * * *

MONICA: Hey, Rach. How would you like some Tiki Death Punch?

RACHEL: What's that?

MONICA: Well, it's rum, and . . .

RACHEL: Okay!

MONICA'S TIKI DEATH PUNCH

Inspired by: "The One With George Stephanopoulos"

Here are two ways to make a big batch of Monica's Tiki Death Punch—one with alcohol, one without, but both equally refreshing.

— SERVES 6 TO 8 —

SPIKED

4¼ ounces lime juice

8 ounces frozen strawberries

16 ounces frozen pineapple chunks

2½ tablespoons granulated sugar

5½ ounces black rum

5½ ounces gold rum

5½ ounces light rum

VIRGIN

8 ounces store-bought lemonade

8 ounces water

4¼ ounces lime juice

8 ounces frozen strawberries

16 ounces frozen pineapple chunks

2½ tablespoons granulated sugar

FOR BOTH:

Mix all the ingredients together in a blender until smooth. Serve straight from a blender or from a pitcher into juice glasses or mason jars and garnish with a lime wedge or strawberry.

Reusable straws optional.

MULLED APPLE CIDER

Inspired by: "The One Where Underdog Gets Away"

Mulled cider is a special holiday treat to sip while your turkey is roasting or other entrées are baking—and it will make your house smell amazing. Try adding orange slices or cored apple slices, which sweeten the mixture and pair well with the spices. It's best to use fresh apple cider, sold seasonally, or unfiltered apple juice. Don't use clear apple juice. If you decide to spike your cider, make sure to add the rum after the mixture has been cooking for a while so it doesn't burn off.

SERVES 16

1 gallon fresh apple cider or unfiltered apple juice

5-6 cinnamon sticks, plus additional for garnishes

10 cloves

1 teaspoon ground nutmeg

1 orange, cut into ¼-inch-thick rounds, plus additional for garnishes

1½ cups Captain Morgan Spiced Rum (optional)

In a large stockpot on the stovetop, warm the apple cider on high heat until it starts to bubble, 8 to 10 minutes.

Once the cider begins to bubble, turn the temperature down to low and add the cinnamon sticks, cloves, nutmeg, and orange slices.

Cover and simmer on low for 1½ hours or more to allow the flavors to meld, creating a smooth, balanced drink.

If adding alcohol to the mixture, add the rum and continue to cook on low for another 30 minutes. Alternatively, let your friends stir the rum into their own mugs.

Ladle into mugs while hot. Garnish with a cinnamon stick or orange slice.

"Okay, cider's mulling, turkey's turkeying, yams are yamming."
—Monica Geller

THE ONE WITH ALL THE FOOD

JENNIFER ANISTON MADE enchiladas for Jimmy Fallon at her 2019 Friendsgiving party. Having some nontraditional Thanksgiving food on your menu is a great way to ensure you and your friends don't get tired of turkey too soon. And for the Joey in you, it's also a good "warm-up" for the big event. That's why, in addition to your classic Thanksgiving fare—turkey, stuffing, and "I Hate Rachel Green" Club Yams—you'll find some nontraditional *Friends*-inspired dishes here, like lasagna, meatball subs, and Righteous Mac 'n' Cheese. And remember, even though "Joey doesn't share food," you and your friends should share and enjoy everything!

MONICA'S CLASSIC ROAST TURKEY

Inspired by: "The One With the Rumor"

Cooking a whole turkey can seem intimidating, but it's actually not hard if you take it step by step, give it a whole lotta love and devotion, and baste the hell out of it. Many recipes suggest basting with butter, but butter burns at a high temperature and can create a smoky oven, so it's best to use extra-virgin olive oil and make a paste with some flavorful seasonings. Roasting low and slow as described in this method will yield a succulent turkey. It's also recommended that you get a turkey baster for basting, which is much easier than trying to wedge a spoon under the rack. Please don't attempt to eat an entire turkey in one sitting like Joey.

SERVES 12 TO 14

1 (12- to 14-pound) frozen turkey, thawed

1 tablespoon salt, plus more for seasoning the turkey

1 teaspoon freshly ground black pepper, plus more for seasoning the turkey

4 ribs celery

2 medium carrots

1 yellow onion

3 tablespoons extra-virgin olive oil, plus more if needed

2 teaspoons dried thyme

2 teaspoons dried sage

1 teaspoon paprika

1 bunch fresh thyme

1 bunch fresh sage

1–2 cups chicken stock or water, plus more if needed

Friendsgiving Gravy (see page 31)

MONICA: You're telling me you can eat almost an entire turkey in one sitting?

JOEY: That's right, 'cause I'm a Tribbiani, and this is what we do. We may not be great thinkers or world leaders, we don't read a lot or run very fast, but damn it we can eat!

The first order of business when roasting a turkey is to clean and dry it thoroughly. To save time, do this the day before you plan to cook it. Remove the giblets and neck from the turkey cavity and save them for later if you're going to use them; otherwise, discard. Then, place the turkey in a roasting pan and season it on all sides with the salt and pepper. For crispier skin, chef Ina Garten recommends leaving the turkey uncovered in the refrigerator overnight. As she explains in her recipe for Make-Ahead Roast Turkey, this will allow the skin to dry out and turn a little translucent.

When you're ready to cook, preheat the oven to 350°F and set the turkey in the pan on the counter. The turkey will be moist after being in the fridge, so dry it completely by blotting it with paper towels, top, bottom, inside, and outside.

Slice the celery crosswise into half-moons. Peel the carrots and cut them into chunks. Peel the onion and cut it into quarters. Set the vegetables aside.

In a small bowl, stir the olive oil, salt, pepper, thyme, sage, and paprika to make a paste.

Put the turkey on a work surface and, using your hands, rub the paste over the turkey to completely coat that baby! This is important—you want to slather the paste over and under the skin thoroughly, but without ripping it.

Gently place the fresh thyme and sage inside the cavity, along with the quartered onion. Don't stuff them!

Add the stock or water and the chopped veggies to the bottom of the roasting pan.

Put a wire rack in the roasting pan and set the turkey on the rack, so no part of the turkey touches the bottom of the pan. This will allow the turkey to crisp on both the top and bottom. If you're feeling confident in the kitchen like Monica, tie the legs together with butcher's twine and tuck the wings under the breasts.

Roast, uncovered, for about 2 and a half hours or more, basting every 30 minutes. (If your bird is larger or smaller, figure about 13 minutes per pound.)

Whenever you baste, make sure there is always some liquid left in the bottom of the pan so the vegetables don't burn. Add more stock or water if needed.

Start checking for doneness during the last 45 minutes of roasting. The turkey is done when a meat thermometer inserted mid-thigh reads 165°F, per Ina Garten (and Mark Bittman). Place the pan on top of your stove and carefully tilt the turkey, still on the rack in the pan, to let the juices run out of the cavity and mix in with the vegetables.

Transfer the turkey to a platter but don't carve it until it has rested for at least 15 minutes to allow the juices to set. Serve with Friendsgiving Gravy.

FRIENDSGIVING GRAVY

Turkey gravy is basically stock and flour. You can include the juices from your turkey once it's done cooking (just strain them through a fine-mesh sieve to remove the cooked vegetables), or if you want to make the gravy ahead of time, then just use turkey or chicken stock. Feel free to be creative and add a little orange juice or wine to your gravy too.

4 cups turkey or chicken stock plus juices from the pan (see note above)

⅓ cup all-purpose flour

Salt and pepper

Put the stock in a saucepan and bring to a boil over medium-high heat. Add the flour and stir until thoroughly combined. Simmer for 10 to 15 minutes or until the gravy has thickened and the flour is fully incorporated. Season with salt and pepper.

MONICA'S LASAGNA FOR CARNIVORES

Inspired by: "The One With the Dozen Lasagnas"

Lasagna is a great dish to make for a potluck-style Friendsgiving! It feeds a crowd. It reheats easily. And it freezes well. If you've never made one before, the trick is letting the big cooked noodles dry flat before assembly. Everyone does the layers a little differently, but however you decide to do it, lasagna's a lot of fun to prepare. It's recommended you make one at a time, even if your favorite Aunt Sylvia asks for a dozen.

——— SERVES 8 TO 10 ———

12–15 lasagna noodles, uncooked

Salt

1 tablespoon extra-virgin olive oil, plus a little for drizzling

1½ pounds ground beef

4 teaspoons garlic powder, divided

2 teaspoons onion powder

2 teaspoons dried oregano

1 teaspoon dried basil

Freshly ground black pepper

1½–2 cups marinara sauce

2 cups whole milk ricotta

1½ cups freshly grated Parmesan, divided

¼ cup chopped fresh parsley

2 cups grated mozzarella cheese

Preheat the oven to 350°F.

Spray a 13 × 9-inch casserole dish with cooking spray.

In a large stockpot, boil the lasagna noodles with a pinch of salt until cooked, according to the package directions, 4 to 5 minutes. Stir frequently to avoid the noodles sticking together. Depending on the size of your pot and how many noodles you want, you may need to cook the noodles in batches.

Drain the noodles in a colander and lay them flat on paper towels to absorb the excess water. Once dry, you can drizzle a little olive oil on the noodles and rub it on gently to keep them from drying out.

"Aunt Syl, stop yelling! All I'm saying is that if you had told me vegetarian lasagna, I would have made vegetarian lasagna. . . . Well, the meat's only every third layer, maybe you could scrape."

—Monica Geller

In a large skillet, heat the oil and brown the ground beef until no longer pink. Add 2 teaspoons of the garlic powder, the onion powder, oregano, basil, 1 teaspoon salt, and ½ teaspoon pepper. Drain the fat and add the marinara sauce to coat the beef. Stir until well combined.

In a medium bowl, combine the ricotta, ½ cup of the Parmesan, the remaining 2 teaspoons of garlic powder, and the parsley. Season with a dash of salt and pepper.

Cover the bottom of your prepared casserole dish with half of the meat sauce. Top with 5 or 6 lasagna noodles placed lengthwise and layered in the pan. The noodles should fit snugly. Then top with a layer of the ricotta mixture. Add a second layer of noodles, the remaining meat sauce, and the ricotta mixture. For the last layer, add a noodle layer and top with the mozzarella and remaining 1 cup Parmesan. Feel free to sprinkle some seasoning on top of the cheese, such as garlic powder and oregano, to give it extra flavor.

Cover with foil, slightly tented (to avoid touching the noodles and cheese), and bake for 30 minutes. Uncover and bake an additional 10 to 15 minutes, until the cheese is slightly browned and bubbly. Let cool before serving.

THE JOEY SPECIAL
HOMEMADE PIZZA

Inspired by: "The One With Ross's Wedding—Part I"

Pizza is one of the most enjoyable meals to make as a group at Friendsgiving. Consider it a good alternative to turkey, especially if you've got some vegetarian eaters coming over or want to offer a highly customizable option for your friends. A great way to go is an individual pizza for each person and a toppings bar. Below is a complete recipe with homemade dough to make one 10- to 12-inch pizza or two 5-inch pizzas . . . feel free to buy ready-made dough, though—we won't tell. Either way, you get to roll the dough and toss it up in the air like a pizza pro! (If you're coordinated like that.)

SERVES 2

1 teaspoon honey

¾ cup warm water

1 teaspoon active dry yeast

1½ cups all-purpose flour, divided

½ teaspoon salt

1 tablespoon olive oil, plus more for greasing and brushing

1 24-ounce jar or container of your favorite pizza sauce

1½ cups shredded fresh or packaged mozzarella cheese

OPTIONAL TOPPINGS OF YOUR CHOICE, SUCH AS:

Italian pork or chicken sausage (This is the only topping you need to cook in advance. Gently sauté in a pan. If the sausage has casing, remove before cooking.)

pepperoni slices

pitted black olives

chopped onions

chopped bell peppers

diced ham

chunks of pineapple

fresh basil leaves

Dissolve the honey in the warm water and stir in the yeast. Let it sit for 5 minutes, or until foamy.

In a large bowl, mix 1 cup of the flour and the salt. Add the yeast mixture and olive oil and mix with a wooden spoon to make a sticky dough.

Turn the dough out onto a floured surface and knead, working in the remaining ½ cup flour, until the dough is soft but no longer sticks, about 5 minutes.

JOEY: You ordered pizza without me?
PHOEBE: We ordered the Joey Special.
JOEY: Two pizzas?!

Shape the dough into a ball and place in an oiled bowl; cover and let rise until approximately doubled in volume, about 1 hour.

Preheat the oven to 450°F.

Punch down the dough. On a lightly floured surface, with a floured rolling pin, roll out the dough into a 10- to 12-inch round. Or cut the dough in half, shape each half into a ball, and roll each piece into a 5-inch round.

Oil a baking sheet or pizza tray with olive oil or cooking spray and transfer the dough to the pan. Brush the dough with a little bit of olive oil (optional).

Ladle sauce onto the center of the pizza and spread it outwards, leaving a good inch of crust sauce-free. Sprinkle the mozzarella on evenly. Add more toppings of choice, if desired.

Bake for 8 to 10 minutes, until the cheese is bubbling. Or, for a crispier crust, bake the dough without toppings for 7 minutes, then add the toppings and bake for an additional 5 to 8 minutes, until the cheese is melted and the crust is browned.

Let cool slightly, slice with a pizza slicer, and transfer to plates.

JOEY'S MEATBALL SUB

Inspired by: "The One With the Ride Along"

Meatball subs are another fun alternative to the usual turkey at Friends-giving. You can prepare the meatballs in advance on your own or with a friend, then let your guests put together their own meatball subs. Some may want them cheesier than others! You'll want to have a vegetarian option as well, such as Grilled Cheese Light and Dark (page 57) or provide some "meatless" meatballs. Just keep in mind, this recipe is so amazing, you might find yourself feeling as protective of your meatball sub as Joey.

SERVES 6

2 tablespoons olive oil, divided

½ onion, diced

1 pound ground beef

½ cup plain breadcrumbs

1 teaspoon minced garlic

1 egg, lightly beaten

1 tablespoon Worcestershire sauce

2 teaspoons salt

1 teaspoon freshly ground black pepper

1 teaspoon dried Italian herb seasoning

1 teaspoon onion powder

1 teaspoon garlic powder

1 teaspoon dried oregano

2 tablespoons grated Parmesan cheese

1 24-ounce jar or container of your favorite marinara sauce

6 fresh Italian sandwich rolls, sliced open

12 slices fresh mozzarella (about 8 ounces)

Heat 1 tablespoon of the olive oil in a small pan over medium heat. Add the onion and cook until translucent. Set aside on a plate.

Preheat the oven to 350°F.

In a large bowl, combine the meat, breadcrumbs, garlic, egg, Worcestershire sauce, salt and pepper, Italian seasoning, onion powder, garlic powder, oregano, and Parmesan. Mix together thoroughly using your hands. Add the onions and mix to combine.

Shape the meat into 1½-inch meatballs and set them aside on a large piece of wax paper or a plate.

Heat the remaining tablespoon of olive oil in a large skillet. Working in batches if necessary, add the meatballs and brown them on all sides.

"I wasn't trying to save Ross, okay? My sandwich was next to Ross. Alright? I was trying to save my sandwich."
—Joey Tribbiani

Transfer the meatballs to a 13 × 9-inch baking dish. Pour in your marinara sauce and cover the pan with aluminum foil. Bake for 1 hour until the meatballs feel very tender.

Preheat the broiler to high.

Line two baking sheets with foil and place 3 rolls, opened flat, on each. Remove some of the bread filling from the inside of each roll so the meatballs will fit.

Add 3 meatballs to the bottom half of each roll and top with some of the sauce, then add two slices of mozzarella cheese. Broil for 3 minutes until the cheese is melted and serve.

"I HATE RACHEL GREEN" CLUB YAMS

Inspired by: "The One With the Rumor"

It simply wouldn't be Thanksgiving without candied yams. Melted marshmallows are optional but obviously heavenly. If you include them, please make sure to do it the Monica way and put them in "concentric circles."

— SERVES 6 TO 8 —

2 pounds sweet potatoes (about 4 large or 6 medium)

⅓ cup granulated sugar or packed brown sugar

3 tablespoons orange juice

3 tablespoons unsalted butter

½ teaspoon vanilla extract

½ teaspoon salt

¼ teaspoon ground cinnamon

3 cups mini marshmallows (optional)

Bring a large pot of water to a boil. Wash the sweet potatoes and score them, then add them to the pot. Cover and boil for about 30 minutes, until the potatoes are easily pierced with a fork.

"Rachel Green . . . God, I hate her, Ross. I hate her. Look at her standing there with those yams. My two greatest enemies, Ross. Rachel Green and complex carbohydrates."
—Will from high school (guest star Brad Pitt)

Drain the potatoes and let them cool in a bowl of cold water for 10 minutes. Peel them (once cooled, the skin should peel right off).

Preheat the oven to 350°F.

Spray an 8 × 8-inch baking dish with cooking spray. Chop the sweet potatoes into ½-inch chunks and place them into the prepared dish.

Combine the sugar, orange juice, butter, vanilla, salt, and cinnamon in a small saucepan and bring to a boil. Pour the sauce over the sweet potatoes and top with the marshmallows, if using.

WILL: We had a club.

RACHEL: You had a club?

WILL: That's right. The "I Hate Rachel Green" Club.

RACHEL: So you all just joined together to hate me? Who else was in this club?

WILL: Me . . . and Ross.

Bake for 20 minutes or until the marshmallows are golden brown, or 10 minutes if you skipped the marshmallows.

STUFFING FOR HUMANS

Inspired by: "The One Where Chandler Doesn't Like Dogs"

If you swear by boxed stuffing (maybe with the addition of some fresh veggies), that's all about to change. Once you learn to make stuffing from scratch, you'll never go back to the boxed stuff! The key is to first bake the bread cubes on a low temperature, tossing them frequently so they toast lightly but don't burn. During this step, you'll actually be making homemade croutons! You won't believe how delicious this smells when it's baking in the oven. If you want to share your masterpiece with your pets, that's your call!

SERVES 10 TO 12

¾ loaf white bread, sourdough, or baguette

2 tablespoons unsalted butter, plus more for greasing

1 Vidalia onion, diced

4 ribs celery, chopped

2 carrots, chopped

2 teaspoons dried sage

2 teaspoons dried thyme

1 teaspoon salt, plus more if needed

½ teaspoon freshly ground black pepper, plus more if needed

1–1½ cups chicken or vegetable stock

Juice of 1 orange

Preheat the oven to 225°F.

Cut the bread up into ¼-inch cubes the size of croutons, leaving the crust on (it adds nice texture).

Grease a 13 × 9-inch baking pan with butter.

"Uh-oh, we left Joey alone with the food . . . There he is . . . feeding stuffing to a dog!"
—Monica Geller

Add the chunks of bread to the pan and bake it for 1 hour, tossing the bread around every 20 minutes to make sure it cooks evenly and the edges darken. Remove from the oven when lightly golden.

In a large pan, melt the butter over medium-high heat and sauté the vegetables until the onions are translucent and the celery and carrots are slightly softened, 3 to 5 minutes. Add the sage and thyme and cook another 1 to 2 minutes, then season with the salt and pepper. Set aside to cool.

In a large bowl, toss together the toasted bread and the vegetables. Pour in the stock gradually until the mixture is wet but not soggy; you may not use all the stock. Add the freshly squeezed orange juice. Mix to combine and add a dash more salt and pepper if needed.

Transfer the stuffing mix back to the baking pan. Bake for about 45 minutes, or until the top is light golden brown and the inside is nice and hot. Let cool and then cover until ready to eat.

MONICA: No! Everything's cold. The turkey's dried out and the . . . the stuffing is all soggy.

CHANDLER: Yeah, and there's a bowl of cranberry sauce that . . . (whispers to Monica) what happens to cranberry sauce?

MONICA: Nothing. It's fine.

CHANDLER: Oh thank God!

CHANBERRY COMPOTE

Inspired by: "The One With the Late Thanksgiving"

It was a big deal when Chandler made cranberries . . . for Chandler, that is. Making cranberry sauce is easy. A great way to spice it up is to add fruit to the cranberries as you cook them, which makes it more like a compote. You can also add dried fruit and nuts if you really want to go crazy. Best of all, you can actually make this recipe up to a week ahead of time and it will stay good in the refrigerator.

SERVES 10

1 cup granulated sugar

1 large apple, peeled and chopped into ½-inch pieces

2 medium pears, peeled and chopped into ½-inch pieces

Zest of ½ an orange

¼ cup orange juice

1 (12-ounce) bag fresh cranberries

In a large pot, bring 1½ cups water and the sugar to a boil. Add the apples, pears, orange zest, and orange juice. Simmer the fruit for 5 minutes, uncovered.

Stir in the cranberries and cook on medium-high heat for 7 to 10 minutes, stirring occasionally, until the berries start to pop but are still whole.

Transfer the compote to a bowl to cool, then chill in the refrigerator until ready to serve.

MRS. GELLER'S LUMPY MASHED POTATOES

Inspired by: "The One Where Underdog Gets Away"

Whether you like mashed potatoes with lumps or without, this simple mashed potato recipe is sure to please—milk, butter, salt, and pepper, with a dash of paprika. No whipping needed, just some good old-fashioned potato mashing. It's delightful and creamy, with or without the lumps.

— SERVES 8 TO 10 —

4 pounds Yukon gold potatoes

½ cup (1 stick) unsalted butter, cut into cubes

¼ teaspoon salt

⅛ teaspoon freshly ground black pepper

1–1½ cups whole milk

¼ teaspoon paprika or chives, for sprinkling

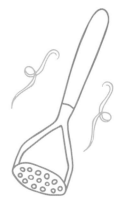

Set a large stockpot of water on the stove to boil. Peel the skin off the potatoes and cut them into 1-inch cubes. To keep the potatoes from browning, place the skinned, cubed potatoes into a large bowl of cold water as you cut them.

Add the cubed potatoes carefully to the boiling water. Boil for about 12 minutes or until the potatoes feel tender when you test them with a fork.

Drain them through a colander, then return the potatoes to the pot. While the pot is still hot, add the butter and stir it into the potatoes until combined.

MONICA: I tell you what, how about I cook dinner at my place? I'll make it just like Mom's.

ROSS: Will you make the mashed potatoes with the lumps?

MONICA: You know they're not actually supposed to . . . I'll work on the lumps.

Using a potato masher, mash the potatoes until they start to form a smooth consistency. (This is the part where you can create lumps if you want. Just don't mash the potatoes completely—leave a few clumps.) Add the salt and pepper and continue to stir.

Gradually add the milk and continue to mash or stir with a spoon until the milk is fully incorporated and the potatoes have a smooth texture (if that's what you're going for). Top with a sprinkling of paprika or chives.

RIGHTEOUS MAC 'N' CHEESE

Inspired by: "The One With All the Thanksgivings"

Sure, you could make boxed macaroni and cheese from the store and toss in a slice of American cheese, but why not do it up for real with an impressive batch of *righteous* mac 'n' cheese? This recipe can also be prepared with the addition or substitution of other kinds of cheese, such as American and Monterey Jack, or you can take it up a notch with fresh Gruyère and medium-sharp cheddar as we've suggested below. Even though buying pre-shredded saves time and energy, it will come out much creamier if you use blocks of cheese and grate the cheese yourself. Pre-shredded cheese has a coating that prevents it from melting well, but you can use pre-shredded Parmesan for the breadcrumb topping. This is a rich, creamy recipe that's perfect to serve at a potluck or anytime you're craving some homemade macaroni and cheese.

SERVES 8 TO 10

FOR THE MACARONI AND CHEESE

1 1-pound (16-ounce) box of elbow pasta

1 tablespoon extra-virgin olive oil

4 cups grated medium-sharp cheddar cheese

2 cups grated Gruyère cheese

½ cup (1 stick) unsalted butter

½ cup all-purpose flour

2½ cups whole milk

1½ cups heavy whipping cream

½ tablespoon salt

½ teaspoon freshly ground black pepper

"Monica, I was wondering if you could make me some of that righteous mac 'n' cheese like last year."

—Chandler Bing

FOR THE PANKO BREADCRUMB TOPPING

4 tablespoons unsalted butter, melted

1½ cups panko bread crumbs

½ cup shredded Parmesan cheese (you can buy pre-shredded)

¼ teaspoon paprika

Preheat the oven to 325°F and spray a 13 × 9-inch casserole dish with cooking spray.

Bring a large pot of water to a boil. Add the pasta and set your timer to cook the pasta until al dente, about 7 minutes. Drain the pasta and pour it into a large bowl. Toss with a little olive oil to prevent sticking and set aside.

Toss together the cheddar and Gruyère. Divide the shredded cheese into four piles (1½ cups per pile), which you will use for the sauce, the inside layer of the casserole, and the topping.

Melt the butter in a large saucepan over medium heat. Add the flour and whisk well to create a roux. Gradually pour in the milk and heavy cream while continuing to whisk. Continue to heat, stirring occasionally, until the white sauce becomes thick.

Stir in the salt and pepper and 1½ cups (one pile) of the grated cheeses. Allow the cheese to melt into the sauce. Stir in another 1½ cups of cheese until fully incorporated.

Pour the cheese sauce into the bowl containing the pasta, scraping the saucepan with a spatula to make sure you get every bit of sauce. Gently mix until the cheese sauce fully coats the pasta.

Pour half of the pasta mixture into the casserole dish and spread it out with a spatula to form an even layer. Top with 1½ cups of grated cheeses (the third pile of cheese), then pour the remaining pasta mixture on top and spread it out evenly.

Sprinkle the top of the casserole with the last 1½ cups of cheese. Set aside on the stovetop.

Make the breadcrumb topping: Melt the butter in a medium bowl in the microwave. Add the panko bread crumbs, Parmesan cheese, and paprika and stir to combine. Sprinkle the topping over the macaroni and cheese.

Bake for 20 to 25 minutes, until the topping is golden brown and the cheese is bubbly.

FANCY RESTAURANT SALAD
WITH GOAT CHEESE, PEARS, AND CANDIED PECANS
Inspired by: "The One With Five Steaks and an Eggplant"

If you're a salad lover, you'll definitely want to know how to make a fancy restaurant salad at home for your Friendsgiving meal. Here's the secret: Everything looks more impressive with a fancy presentation. If you're serving buffet-style to a group, layer the sliced pears around the outer edge of the bowl, with dressing served on the side. If you're preparing individual salad plates, stack the pear slices at an angle on the side of each plate and drizzle a little dressing for effect.

You can pair this salad with a champagne vinaigrette to bring out the sweetness of the nuts and cranberries, as described below, but it can also be done with a balsamic dressing for something more tart. Don't toss the salad ahead of time because you don't want the lettuce to wilt. P.S. Please don't confuse this salad with the "dirty" one that Monica was asked to make in a different episode. This is a *clean*, fancy salad, and it's good enough to serve as an entrée too, not just to the side of your water!

SERVES 4 TO 6

FOR THE CHAMPAGNE VINAIGRETTE

⅓ cup champagne vinegar

2 teaspoons Dijon mustard

1 small lemon, juiced

1 teaspoon minced garlic

1 teaspoon honey

¼ teaspoon salt

¼ teaspoon freshly ground black pepper

½ cup extra-virgin olive oil

FOR THE SALAD

7 ounces fresh mixed
spring greens

1 cup chopped, candied
pecans (see recipe below)

⅓ cup sweetened, dried
cranberries

4 ounces crumbled goat
cheese

2 pears, preferably Anjou
or Bartlett, cored and
thinly sliced

FOR THE CANDIED PECANS

½ cup packed brown sugar

¼ teaspoon salt

¼ teaspoon ground
cinnamon

1 cup pecan halves

MAKE THE VINAIGRETTE

Add the vinegar, mustard, lemon juice, garlic, honey, salt, and pepper to a
mixing bowl or salad dressing shaker and whisk or shake together. Pour in the
olive oil gradually and whisk or shake until combined.

MAKE THE SALAD

Place the greens in a large serving bowl. Toss the nuts, cranberries, and goat
cheese with the greens.

Layer the sliced pears around the outer edge of the bowl for a "fancy restaurant"
look, and serve the dressing on the side. Or, if plating individually, put a mound
of salad on each plate and stack pear slices on the edge; drizzle each salad with
a little dressing.

MAKE THE CANDIED PECANS

In a small saucepan, combine the brown sugar, salt, cinnamon, and 2 tablespoons
water and cook over medium heat, occasionally scraping down the sides of the
pan with a spatula, until the sugar dissolves and the syrup starts to bubble. Add
the pecans and cook for about 3 minutes until they are fully glazed.

Remove the glazed pecans and spread them out on a piece of parchment
paper to cool for 1 hour. They will be slightly sticky at first but the sugar glaze
will harden as they cool. These may be made ahead and stored in an airtight
container for up to 2 weeks.

RACHEL: I will have the side salad.
WAITER: And what will that be on the side of?
RACHEL: I don't know. Why don't you put it right here next to my water?

SEXY CARAMELIZED CARROTS

Inspired by: "The One With All the Thanksgivings"

When this honey-butter glaze caramelizes in the oven, it transforms ordinary carrots into something extraordinary. This side dish complements just about any meal and can be seasoned with a sprinkling of fresh herbs such as rosemary, thyme, or parsley. Also, while you can substitute bagged, pre-cut carrots in a pinch, they won't have as much flavor and are sometimes bitter, so stick with fresh ones. They're sexy anyway.

— SERVES 8 TO 10 —

2 pounds fresh carrots

¼ cup (½ stick) unsalted butter

2 tablespoons honey

1 teaspoon salt

⅛ teaspoon freshly ground black pepper

⅓ cup chopped fresh parsley or your choice of herbs

Preheat the oven to 375°F. Line two baking sheets with foil and coat the foil with cooking spray.

Peel the carrots. If you're using larger carrots, cut them on a diagonal into ½-inch-thick slices. If you're using smaller carrots, leave the carrots whole with the greens still attached, if possible, for a nice presentation. Place the carrots on the baking sheets in a single layer.

In a small saucepan over low heat, heat the butter until it becomes slightly brown (watch carefully as this happens quickly). Stir in the honey, salt, and pepper. Remove the pan from the heat. Pour the glaze over the carrots and toss to coat.

"I love carrots. Sometimes I like to put them between my fingers like this and hold them down here while I talk to you."

—Monica Geller

Roast the carrots, tossing them about halfway through cooking, until they are caramelized and easily pierced through with a fork, about 30 minutes. Cooking time will vary depending on the size of your carrots. Garnish with fresh parsley before serving.

PHOEBE'S ROGUE EGGPLANT APPETIZER

Inspired by: "The One With Five Steaks and an Eggplant"

After watching this episode, you might have a sudden urge to grill steak and make eggplant. This tangy eggplant recipe also makes a welcome complement to your heavier Friendsgiving fare, so it's a great side to whip up and add to the mix.

——— SERVES 8 TO 10 ———

2 large eggplants

1 tablespoon olive oil

¼ cup red wine vinegar

1 teaspoon salt

½ teaspoon freshly ground black pepper

1 red pepper, diced

½ cucumber, cut lengthwise into quarters then chopped

1 medium red onion, finely diced

4 radishes, thinly sliced then stacked and quartered

Preheat the oven to 400°F.

Pierce the eggplants' skin in several places. Roast the whole eggplants on a baking sheet for about 35 to 45 minutes, or until they are soft and collapsed.

Let the eggplants cool, then slice them in half lengthwise. Use a fork to scoop out the flesh, separating it from the skin. Throw away the skin. Chop the eggplant flesh, then place it into a large glass or wooden bowl (some metal discolors eggplant).

CHANDLER: Hey, stick a fork in me, I am done.

PHOEBE: Stick a fork what?

CHANDLER: Like when you're cooking steak.

PHOEBE: Oh, okay, I don't eat meat.

CHANDLER: Well then how do you know when vegetables are done?

PHOEBE: Well you don't. You just, you eat them and you can tell.

CHANDLER: Oh, okay, well then eat me, I'm done.

Add the oil, vinegar, salt, and black pepper and mix well. Add the red pepper, cucumber, onion, and radishes and stir to evenly distribute.

Cover the bowl tightly and refrigerate overnight. Serve with your favorite crackers.

CHANDLER: Shall I carve?

RACHEL: By all means.

CHANDLER: Okay, who wants light cheese, and who wants dark cheese?

ROSS: I don't even want to know about the dark cheese.

GRILLED CHEESE LIGHT AND DARK

Inspired by: "The One Where Underdog Gets Away"

When Monica burns the turkey and the gang eats grilled cheese for Thanksgiving, this is actually a great lesson. If you mess something up in the kitchen, don't let it ruin your party. There's usually something you can pull together with little effort, like grilled cheese or omelettes. Speaking of grilled cheese, here's a pro tip: A combination of mayonnaise and butter on the outside of the bread creates a richer, crispier sandwich—truly a winning duo whether you prefer your sandwich light or dark.

SERVES 1

1 tablespoon unsalted butter, divided

1 tablespoon mayonnaise

2 slices white bread

4 slices of your favorite cheese (about 2 ounces), such as American, cheddar, Muenster, or Swiss

Melt half the butter in a nonstick skillet over medium heat.

Spread the mayonnaise on one side of each slice of bread.

Once the butter melts, place 1 slice of bread, mayonnaise side down, in the skillet and top with the cheese, then add the second piece of bread, mayonnaise side up.

For a darker sandwich, flip it after about 4 minutes, add the remaining butter to the pan, and cook for another 2 to 3 minutes, until the cheese is melted.

For a lighter sandwich, flip the sandwich after 2 minutes and follow the steps above.

THE MOIST MAKER

Inspired by: "The One With Ross's Sandwich"

Never underestimate the power of a really good sandwich! This one might sound a bit unappealing at first, but wait until you try it. It's actually really good! The trick is to just lightly dip the middle piece of bread in the gravy to avoid a soggy sandwich.

SERVES 1

3 slices white bread

Mayonnaise (optional)

Friendsgiving Gravy (page 31)

Roasted turkey breast, sliced

Stuffing for Humans (page 40) or other leftover stuffing

Chanberry Compote (page 43) or cranberry sauce

Lightly toast two slices of bread.

Spread a dollop of mayonnaise (if using) onto each piece of toast.

Heat a small bowl of gravy in the microwave or on the stovetop. Add a little water as leftover refrigerated gravy thickens.

Dip the third piece of bread in the hot gravy to coat, then quickly take it out and set aside. Let the excess gravy drip off the bread before you make your sandwich, unless you like it messy (which is also delicious).

Build your sandwich in layers: Bread, turkey, stuffing, cranberries, gravy-soaked bread, then more turkey, stuffing, cranberries, and the top piece of bread.

Cut in half and take the biggest bite you can!

"You see my sister makes these amazing turkey sandwiches. Her secret is, she puts an extra slice of gravy-soaked bread in the middle; I call it the Moist Maker."

—Ross Geller

ROASTED SAVORY BRUSSELS SPROUTS FOR LATECOMERS

Inspired by: "The One With the Late Thanksgiving"

Brussels sprouts often get a bad rep thanks to their stinky smell. But when cooked the right way, they are delicious. The sweet cranberries and creamy blue cheese complement the bitterness of the Brussels sprouts in this sweet and savory side dish.

SERVES 8 TO 10

1 pound Brussels sprouts

2 tablespoons olive oil

2 tablespoons apple cider vinegar

1 teaspoon maple syrup

¼ teaspoon salt

¼ teaspoon freshly ground black pepper

¼ cup dried cranberries

¼ cup crumbled blue cheese (or goat cheese or feta)

Preheat the oven to 400°F .

Trim the Brussels sprouts and cut them in half lengthwise (so they still hold together). Remove any discolored leaves or sprouts.

In a large bowl, whisk together the olive oil, apple cider vinegar, maple syrup, salt, and pepper. Add the Brussels sprouts and toss to coat.

RACHEL: Oh my god, it's Brussels sprouts.
ROSS: That's worse than no food.

Pour the sprouts into a 13 × 9-inch baking pan. Bake for 25 minutes, then remove the pan from the oven and stir the sprouts so they cook evenly. I like to give the pan a good shake.

Cook for another 20 minutes, or until the Brussels sprouts look golden brown and slightly crispy on the outside leaves (which will be darker) and have a healthy green color overall. They should feel tender but still firm when a fork is inserted.

Remove from the oven, add the cranberries and blue cheese, and gently toss to combine. Serve in a nice round or oval serving dish.

⟨ RACHEL'S ⟩
THANKSGIVING TRIFLE

Inspired by: "The One Where Ross Got High"

Making a trifle is no small feat, but it's also majorly rewarding. Since there are many components, it helps to make this dessert with a good friend. A traditional English trifle has three layers of the following: sherry-soaked cake (or ladyfingers) topped with jam, fruit, custard, and whipped cream. The below recipe uses a vanilla cake made from scratch and substitutes homemade vanilla pudding for the custard. But to simplify your trifle, you can use boxed cake (white or yellow) or ladyfingers, and boxed or premade custard or pudding. As long as you leave out the beef, you'll be good to go!

—— SERVES 10 TO 12 ——

FOR THE VANILLA CAKE

1 cup (2 sticks) unsalted butter, at room temperature, plus more for the pans

3 cups all-purpose flour, plus more for the pans

3½ teaspoons baking powder

½ teaspoon salt

1 cup granulated sugar

4 eggs, at room temperature

4 teaspoons vanilla extract

1¼ cups whole milk, at room temperature

½ cup cream sherry

3 heaping tablespoons red raspberry jam

"A layer of ladyfingers, a layer of jam, custard, raspberries, more ladyfingers, beef sautéed with peas and onions, a little more custard, sliced banana, and whipped cream."

—Rachel Green

FOR THE VANILLA PUDDING

1 cup granulated sugar

6 tablespoons cornstarch

½ teaspoon salt

4 cups whole milk

2 tablespoons unsalted butter

2 teaspoons vanilla extract

"It smells like feet."
—Ross Geller

FOR THE FRUIT

2 cups fresh strawberries, sliced, plus more for garnish

1 cup fresh raspberries, plus more for garnish

2 tablespoons cream sherry

1½ tablespoons granulated sugar

FOR THE WHIPPED CREAM

1½ cups heavy whipping cream

1 teaspoon confectioners' sugar

1 teaspoon vanilla extract

MAKE THE CAKE

Preheat the oven to 350°F. Grease and flour two 9-inch round cake pans.

In a medium bowl, sift together the flour, baking powder, and salt.

In a large bowl, cream together the butter and granulated sugar. Beat in the eggs, one at a time, then stir in the vanilla. Beat in the flour mixture alternately with the milk until fully incorporated into the batter. Pour into the prepared pans, dividing the batter evenly.

Bake for 30 to 35 minutes, until the cakes are golden on top and a toothpick inserted into the middle comes out clean. Let cool for 10 to 15 minutes before removing the cakes from the pans.

Once cooled, brush both sides of the cakes with the sherry so they're fully coated. Spread the jam over the top of each cake and cut the cakes into 1-inch wedges.

MAKE THE VANILLA PUDDING

In a medium bowl, whisk together the granulated sugar, cornstarch, and salt. In a large saucepan, heat the milk over medium heat until bubbles form at the edges, stirring constantly to avoid burning. Pour the dry ingredients into the hot milk, a little at a time, stirring to dissolve. Continue to cook and stir for about 15 minutes, stirring constantly to avoid burning, until the pudding mixture thickens. Do not let it boil.

Remove from the heat and stir in the butter and vanilla. Chill in the refrigerator for at least 1 hour.

MAKE THE FRUIT

In a medium bowl, combine the strawberries, raspberries, sherry, and granulated sugar and toss to thoroughly coat the fruit. Allow to macerate (chef-speak for getting soft and liquidy) in the refrigerator until you're ready to assemble the trifle.

MAKE THE WHIPPED CREAM

Combine the cream, confectioners' sugar, and vanilla in a large mixer bowl. Beat on high speed for 2 to 3 minutes until stiff peaks form. Chill in the refrigerator.

ASSEMBLE THE TRIFLE

Place one-third of the cake wedges in the bottom of the trifle dish (jam side facing up). Top with a layer of fruit, a layer of pudding, and a layer of whipped cream. Repeat the layers two more times. Garnish with fresh berries. Cover and chill in the refrigerator until ready to serve.

"What's not to like? Custard: good! Jam: good! Meat: gooooood!"
—Joey Tribbiani

MONICA'S APPLE CRUMBLE

Inspired by: "The One With the Rumor"

Leave it to Joey to still have room for pie after finishing an entire turkey. When it comes to baking, there's nothing better than a delicious dessert recipe that comes together quickly and still looks impressive. Meet the apple crumble—apple pie's best buddy! A crumble is simply a dish of baked, fresh fruit with a streusel crumb topping. Best served warm with a side of vanilla ice cream.

SERVES 6

- ½ cup (1 stick) unsalted butter, cold, plus more for greasing
- 4 Granny Smith apples, peeled if preferred, thinly sliced (3–3½ cups),
- ¼ cup orange juice

- ½ cup packed light brown sugar
- ¾ cup sifted all-purpose flour
- ½ teaspoon ground cinnamon
- ¼ teaspoon ground nutmeg
- Pinch of salt

Preheat the oven to 375°F.

Lightly grease a 9-inch pie plate. Mound the sliced apples in the pie plate. Pour the orange juice all over the apples.

In a medium bowl, mix the sugar, flour, cinnamon, nutmeg, and salt. Slice the cold butter into half-inch chunks, then use two butter knives or a fork to cut it into the flour mixture until it becomes crumbly. Sprinkle the streusel over the apple filling.

Bake for 45 minutes until the streusel is golden brown and the apples are tender.

Serve warm with vanilla ice cream.

REAL CHOCOLATE CHIP CAKE

Inspired by: "The One With the List"

Everyone can breathe a sigh of relief—we won't be using "Mockolate" in this book, so there will be no evil to speak of. This cake tastes nice and light (though there is a lot of butter involved) and uses *real* chocolate chips. It's also made in an angel food cake pan, which creates a nicely shaped cake that always seems to impress.

— SERVES 8 TO 10 —

4 eggs, separated

1 cup (2 sticks) unsalted butter, plus more for greasing

2 cups granulated sugar

2⅔ cups sifted flour

2⅔ teaspoons baking powder

⅛ teaspoon salt

1 cup whole milk

1½ teaspoons vanilla extract

1 12-ounce package mini semisweet chocolate chips (or standard-size semisweet chocolate chips, crushed so they won't sink to the bottom of the cake)

Preheat the oven to 350°F. Grease a 10-inch (16-cup) angel food cake pan (also called a tube pan. Make sure it has a removable bottom.)

Beat the egg whites in a medium bowl until peaks form.

In a large bowl, cream together the butter, sugar, and egg yolks.

Mix together the flour, baking powder, and salt in a small bowl.

"Oh, oh sweet lord, this is what evil must taste like!"
—Phoebe Buffay (upon tasting Monica's Mockolate Chip Cookies)

♡ ♡ ♡ ♡ ♡

Mix the dry ingredients, alternating with the milk, into the creamed butter and sugar mixture in the large bowl. Stir in the vanilla. Fold in the chocolate chips. Fold in the egg whites gently but thoroughly.

Pour the batter into the prepared pan and bake for 1 hour. Test using a toothpick. If the cake is still wet, bake for another 5 to 10 minutes, watching closely, until a toothpick inserted into the center comes out clean.

Let cool for 20 minutes, then gently release the cake from the cake pan onto a plate.

Slice and enjoy!

FLOOR CHEESECAKE

Inspired by: "The One With All the Cheesecakes"

To describe this delectable cheesecake recipe, we'll borrow the words of Rachel Green: "It had a buttery, crumbly, graham cracker crust with a very rich, yet light cream cheese filling." Cheesecake is a nice alternative to the traditional Thanksgiving pie. Eating it off the floor, like Rachel and Chandler did, is not a recommended way to enjoy this recipe (despite its name), but it's soooo good that you might find your friends scraping their plates to savor every last crumb. P.S. It's almost impossible to make homemade cheesecake without getting some cracks. Once your cheesecake is ready to serve, just cover up the cracks with some lovely, fresh berries.

SERVES 10 TO 12

FOR THE CRUST

1¼ cups graham cracker crumbs

3 tablespoons unsalted butter, melted, plus more for greasing

⅓ cup granulated sugar

1 teaspoon ground cinnamon (optional)

FOR THE FILLING

6 eggs

2 pounds cream cheese, at room temperature

2 cups granulated sugar

1 tablespoon vanilla extract

2 pints sour cream

Fresh berries, for garnish

CHANDLER: You can't return a box after you've opened the box.
RACHEL: Why not?
CHANDLER: Because it's too delicious.

"Oh look, there's a piece that doesn't have floor on it."
—Rachel Green

Preheat the oven to 350°F.

MAKE THE CRUST

Mix the graham cracker crumbs, melted butter, sugar, and cinnamon (if using) in a small bowl. Lightly grease a 10-inch round springform pan. Press the crumb mixture firmly into the bottom and 1 inch up the sides of the pan. Put the pan on a baking sheet and bake for 9 to 10 minutes, until set. Let it cool, but leave the oven on.

MAKE THE FILLING

In a medium bowl, gently whip the eggs with a fork. Put the softened cream cheese in a large bowl and beat with an electric mixer until fluffy. Gradually beat in the eggs and sugar until combined. As soon as the eggs are incorporated into the batter, stop mixing to avoid making the cheesecake too dense. Using a spatula, gently fold in the vanilla and sour cream. Pour the cheesecake mixture into the crust.

Bake for 1 hour. Turn off the heat and leave the pan in the oven for 30 minutes. (This allows the cheesecake to set.)

Refrigerate overnight. Serve with fresh berries on top or on the side.

NESLÉ TOULOUSE BROWN BUTTER CHOCOLATE CHIP COOKIES

Inspired by: "The One With Phoebe's Cookies"

Imagine how Monica felt when she learned that the chocolate chip recipe she'd been busting her butt to figure out was none other than the one written on a package of Nestlé Toll House morsels. Here's a recipe that incorporates the richness of these chocolate morsels but adds a unique nutty flavor through the act of browning the butter before adding it to the dough. It's no exaggeration to say these cookies are utterly amazing—which makes them the perfect treat to share with your closest friends at your next Friendsgiving.

———— MAKES 24 COOKIES ————

1 cup (2 sticks) unsalted butter, cut into cubes

1¾ cups all-purpose flour

1½ teaspoons salt

1 teaspoon baking soda

1 cup packed dark brown sugar

½ cup granulated sugar

2 teaspoons vanilla extract

1 egg, at room temperature

1 egg yolk, at room temperature

¾ cup semisweet chocolate chips

Preheat the oven to 350°F. Line two baking sheets with parchment paper.

Brown the butter: In a medium saucepan, melt the butter slowly over medium heat. Once the butter melts, it will start to boil and foam; stir constantly for

PHOEBE: Well, you know, I may have relatives in France who would know. My grandmother said she got the recipe from her grandmother, Neslé Toulouse.

MONICA: What was her name?

PHOEBE: Neslé Toulouse.

MONICA: Nestlé Toll House?

about 5 minutes. As soon as the butter turns slightly brown, remove it from the heat and transfer the brown butter to a glass bowl or measuring cup to cool. Allow it to cool to room temperature, about 20 minutes.

Sift the flour, salt, and baking soda into a small bowl.

In a large bowl, combine the brown sugar, granulated sugar, vanilla, and the brown butter. Using an electric mixer or a wooden spoon, cream together for 1 to 2 minutes. Add the egg and egg yolk and mix to incorporate fully. Add the dry ingredients and mix until combined. Fold in the chocolate chips.

Scoop the batter in large spoonfuls onto the prepared pans. Bake for 10 to 12 minutes, until the cookies are golden brown around the edges.

JOEY'S EASY BROWNIES

Inspired by: "The One Where Joey Dates Rachel"

Don't worry, with this recipe, you'll be serving *whole* brownies. Homemade brownies have a slightly different taste and texture than brownies made from a box mix. These are rich and moist and keep for days when stored in an airtight container. The best part about this recipe is that you can make the whole thing in a single saucepan on the stove before baking. That's why they're called Joey's *Easy* Brownies. Make sure you share them with all your friends at Friendsgiving (instead of keeping them to yourself like Joey would).

MAKES 24 BROWNIES

1 cup (2 sticks) unsalted butter

4 ounces (4 squares) unsweetened baker's chocolate

2 cups granulated sugar

4 eggs

2 teaspoons vanilla extract

1 cup all-purpose unsifted flour

1 cup semisweet chocolate chips

¾ cup chopped walnuts (optional)

Preheat the oven to 350°F. Line a 13 × 9-inch pan with parchment paper. (This makes the brownies easy to lift out of the pan and cut.)

In a large saucepan, melt the butter and baker's chocolate over low heat. Stir in the sugar until dissolved. Whisk in the eggs, one at a time. Add the vanilla and gradually add the flour, mixing until combined.

" . . . And a brownie. Well, half a brownie. Actually, it's just a bag. It was a long walk from the flower shop and I was starting to feel faint."

—Joey Tribbiani

Turn off the heat and fold in the chocolate chips. (If you want to add the walnuts, fold those in as well.) Pour the mixture into the prepared pan.

Bake for 20 to 25 minutes, or until a fork inserted into the center comes out clean. Let cool completely, for at least 30 minutes. Or chill them in the refrigerator to help the brownies bind together more quickly for cutting.

Once cooled, lift the brownies out of the pan and transfer them to a cutting board, with the parchment paper beneath them. Cut into six 2-inch rows. Remove the parchment paper and cut each row into 2-inch squares to make 24 brownies.

MONICA: So I'll get candles and my mom's lace tablecloth and since it's Rachel's birthday and we want it to be special, I thought I'd poach a salmon.

(GROANS from Ross, Joey, Chandler, and Phoebe)

MONICA: What?

ROSS: Question, why do we always have to have parties where you poach things?

MONICA: You want to be in charge of the food committee?

ROSS: Question two, why do we always have to have parties with committees?

⤳ PART TWO ⤳

ENTERTAINING

IS BEING FANCY OVERRATED? You decide. It's your Friendsgiving party and you set the tone. If you want to go fancy like Monica, break out the china. If you'd rather kick back like Joey and Phoebe, keep it casual. You can head up as many (or few) planning committees as you want. Read on and learn how to entertain like a pro for whichever type of *Friends* soiree best suits you.

★ ♪ ⚜ ★

JOEY: Yeah, really, why can't we just get some pizzas and get some beers and have fun?

PHOEBE: Yeah, I agree, I think fancy parties are only fun if you're fancy on the inside and I'm just not sure we are.

MAKING A CHECKLIST

Ross has shown us that a list can serve many purposes. From his celebrity "freebie" list to his pros and cons list comparing Rachel and Julie, Ross's lists didn't always benefit him, but they sure did keep him organized. Maintaining a checklist is a great way to stay on top of things throughout your Friendsgiving planning.

First, a couple of checklist "don'ts" that we learned through Ross:

- Don't laminate it. You may need to "pivot" and make changes.

- Don't write anything negative on it, on the off chance the wrong person might see it.

Now, for the "dos." Here are some things you might want on your checklist:

- Decide what kind of Friendsgiving you're going to host. Basically, you can cook everything the Monica Geller way, go halfsies and cook some things, or go full-on potluck style. If you're a top-notch cook as well as a kickass party planner and you want to do everything yourself, go for it. But it's easier, more cost-effective, and much more fun to host a potluck. You'll also want to decide in advance if you want to have Thanksgiving food or non-Thanksgiving food and if you're going for any specific themes.

Checklist
☑ Invitations
☑ Spreadsheet
☑ Shopping list

- Send a trackable electronic invite with an RSVP deadline so you can get an accurate head count. You've probably figured out by now that using a trackable program will help you keep on top of responses, future notes to your guests, and those pesky, yet necessary, follow-ups.

Ross climbs up the fire escape to read Rachel his "pros" list about her.

- Create a shareable digital spreadsheet (such as a Google Sheet) and have your guests sign up for the dishes they plan to bring. Include the link in your invitation. There's a reason why Chandler got very excited about his computer's spreadsheet capabilities. It eliminates the hard work. Food sign-ups will make everyone accountable to bring something and also ensure you won't get too much of the same food. You can be specific and include suggestions of dishes you'd like to have, or roll the dice and leave it totally up to chance. Don't forget to include yourself on the spreadsheet, and let everyone know what you're planning to cook so no one steals your thunder!

- Make a separate shopping list with everything you need to buy, such as:

  - Recipe ingredients
  - Drinks and alcohol
  - Decorations
  - Cups, plates, napkins

  - Bags of ice (day of party)
  - Miscellaneous supplies needed for party activities

- And, finally, create a timeline of what needs to get done when. Trust me, this will keep you sane.

FRIENDSGIVING PLANNING TIMELINE

A little planning goes a long way . . . and so does some cleaning.

3–4 WEEKS AHEAD:
- [ ] Plan the menu or theme of the potluck
- [ ] Create the spreadsheet
- [ ] Send the invitation

2 WEEKS AHEAD:
- [ ] Get rid of any clutter
- [ ] Tidy up your space

1 WEEK AHEAD:
- [ ] Do follow-ups on RSVPs and potluck items everyone has offered to bring
- [ ] Buy dry ingredients
- [ ] Buy or make DIY decorations (see page 94)
- [ ] Clean! (Make Monica Geller proud.)

1–2 DAYS AHEAD:
- [ ] Reread your recipes
- [ ] Buy the fresh ingredients
- [ ] Review your lists and survey your space to see if there's anything else you need to buy or ask friends to bring. Do you need additional chairs or an extra folding table to serve as a drinks station or buffet?

THE DAY BEFORE:
- [ ] Cook and prep whatever you can the day before! Many of the recipes in this book can be made a whole day ahead and just reheated or finished the day of Friendsgiving. Lasagna, mac 'n' cheese, pizza dough, stuffing, cranberries, and all of the desserts can be made ahead of time.
- [ ] Buy ice (if it fits in your freezer; if not, buy day of or assign to a friend).

ROSS: Okay, I'm done with my choices. These are final.

RACHEL: Well, it's about time.

JOEY: Ooh, very official.

ROSS: Oh, yeah, well, ya know, Chandler printed it up on his computer.

MONICA: And who laminated it?

ROSS: That was me.

RACHEL: Alright, let me see. Uma Thurman, Winona Ryder, Elizabeth Hurley, Michelle Pfeiffer, and . . . Dorothy Hamill?

ROSS: Hey, it's my list.

RACHEL: Okay, honey, you do realize she only spins like that on ice.

THE NIGHT BEFORE:

If you can do these things the night before, it's less you have to worry about on the big day.

☐ Set the table
☐ Do a little decorating

THE DAY OF:

☐ Cook whatever is left to cook, like that big, bad turkey if you're going for it!
☐ Chill drinks (Pour yourself one while you're at it.)
☐ Put on your party pants, playlist, and welcome your friends over!

AMBIANCE À LA MONICA'S APARTMENT

For a truly authentic *Friends*-style event, you'll naturally want to incorporate some shabby chic décor from Monica's apartment. Of course, you may not be ready to commit to a fresh purple paint job and complete refurnishing. The good news is, you don't have to. With a few simple touches, you can decorate your entertaining space with both *Friends* vibes and Thanksgiving spirit.

French Art

The framed French advertisement that hangs above Monica's television is an iconic piece of art on the show. Add some vintage flair to your décor by hanging up one or two French posters of your own. (Hint: You can find Monica's "Jouets" poster online.) Just don't ask Joey how to pronounce anything, as we learned in "The One Where Joey Speaks French."

Catch a hint of the Jouets poster behind the television and Rachel's bridesmaid dress in "The One With Barry and Mindy's Wedding."

Monica's turquoise cabinets have a retro, eclectic feel.

Turquoise Kitchen Accents

Let's get real—you're probably not about to resurface your kitchen cabinets in turquoise. (If you are, right on!) But you could pay homage to Monica's kitchen by displaying some fun, retro turquoise accessories instead, such as vases, dishes, and serveware.

Flowers, Pumpkins, and Candles Everywhere

Fresh flowers, whether from your garden or a store, are a nice touch! Get creative and place them like Monica in little arrangements throughout your space. If you're on a tighter budget, skip the flowers and focus on using some pumpkins (if it's fall) and candles. For the pumpkins, look for both orange and white ones and mix in some gourds if you want to get a little crazy.

Candles are a great way to set the mood. Mix up your styles with pillars and votives. Look for soy and beeswax, which are eco-friendly,

Chandler proposes to Monica by candlelight.
♡ ♡ ♡ ♡ ♡ ♡ ♡ ♡ ♡ ♡ ♡ ♡

Phoebe proudly shows off her dollhouse aroma room before it catches on fire.

and try to find candles on sale. Scented versus unscented is a personal choice; keep in mind that strongly scented candles can give some people a headache. And a note on fire safety—make sure you never leave your "aroma room" unattended. We learned a valuable lesson through Phoebe's unfortunate dollhouse mishap! You can always use LED candles to be safe.

Look closely at Monica's cute but mismatched kitchen chairs.

Mismatched Cushions, Pillows, and Chairs

Nothing actually matches in Monica's apartment and that's exactly the point. As type-A as she is, Monica's style is the opposite of matchy-matchy. In fact, she never has a set of matching kitchen chairs or cushions. So, mix up your cushions, pillows, and throw blankets. If you're feeling extra bold, put some oversized throw pillows around your coffee table or seating area for "chill" time.

Ross demonstrates the "hug and roll" strategy to Chandler using one of Monica's larger sofa cushions.

Monica's living room features purple walls, and her front door will forever be remembered for its uber-iconic yellow peephole frame.

Purple Wallpaper Hacks for Hard-Core Fans

If you have extra time and are up to the task, a good hack to pull off Monica's purple walls is to use peel-and-stick removable wallpaper. Order it online and place it behind your French posters, on the back of your door, or wherever you have space. Then, simply remove it and save it for your next Friendsgiving when you're done. Just make sure you get a brand that's guaranteed not to leave any sticky residue behind.

Another route is to use purple fabric. Hang it on the back of your front door along with a yellow peephole frame and you'll achieve next-level *Friends* status before you know it.

TABLESCAPING

"Tablescaping" is a fancy term for table-setting. Believe it or not, competitive tablescaping is a real thing. Imagine if Monica knew about this? When you're going buffet style, you don't technically need to put down place settings. But a little tablescaping is an ideal opportunity to work in some of the meaning behind Friendsgiving, along with a little *Friends*-esque magic.

The Tablecloth

Monica uses a different tablecloth whenever the gang has a sit-down Thanksgiving dinner. They range in color from hunter green to yellow to patterns of fall leaves or blue checkers. That being said, you have lots of options.

The Centerpiece

A centerpiece is designed to enhance the feeling of an event and should also draw your eye to the table. You can arrange items close together in the center or spread out your décor along the table. Monica uses candles, mini pumpkins and gourds, and flowers to create a warm, inviting, and festive atmosphere in the Thanksgiving episodes.

Revisit the episodes and scroll through some websites

and magazines to get ideas, then go for it and let your own style shine. Here are some possible items to inspire your Friendsgiving centerpiece:

- Pillar candles

- Mini pumpkins

- Leaves and branches

- Small floral arrangements that don't obstruct views and conversation

See page 84 for tips on choosing candles and flowers.

MONICA (re: napkins): Oh, no no no, no sweetie. Not like that. We're not at a barn dance. You want to fold them like swans like I showed you at Christmastime, remember?

PHOEBE: Yeah, it all just came screaming back to me.

"Happy Friendsgiving" Napkin Rings

Create some "Happy Friendsgiving" napkin rings. Open a new Word doc, create a text box, and format it to 7 × 1.5 inches. Choose a font or image and place it in the middle of the text box. Copy and paste the text box a few times, then print and cut into strips. Wrap each strip around a rolled-up napkin. Secure each one with a small piece of Scotch tape.

"What Are You Thankful For?" Place Cards

Thankful place cards are the perfect prompt for reminding each other what you're grateful for. You can easily create the place cards using a free, downloadable template. I used a template from Avery, but you can find lots of sources for them online. Provide a pencil with each card so guests can write down their thoughts and, then later, you can gather them up and use them to play "The Thankful Game" (page 136).

Frame-Worthy Food Quotes

Frame some of the best one-liners about food from the Thanksgiving episodes. We've provided some of our favorites! Put each one in a turquoise frame that's reminiscent of Monica's turquoise cabinets and prop them up on the dining table, the buffet table, and the drinks station.

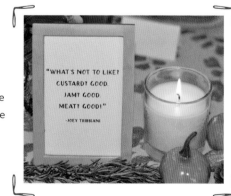

"Don't you put words in people's mouths. You put turkey in people's mouths."
—Joey Tribbiani

"I wasn't supposed to put beef in the trifle."
—Rachel Green

"Someone ate the only good thing in my life."
—Ross Geller

"You want to put the marshmallows in concentric circles."
—Monica Geller

"What's not to like? Custard: good! Jam: good! Meat: goooood!"
—Joey Tribbiani

DINNERWARE AND BUFFET-STYLE SERVING

Fancy china is lovely if you're hosting a formal dinner and prepared to wash a whole bunch of dishes afterward, while taking extra measures not to chip them. The best thing about a Friendsgiving potluck is that it's casual, so unless you're committed to using real plates, take a load off and heed this advice.

Opt for Disposable Dinnerware

Palm-leaf and bamboo tableware are both eco-friendly options. You can order them in bulk online.

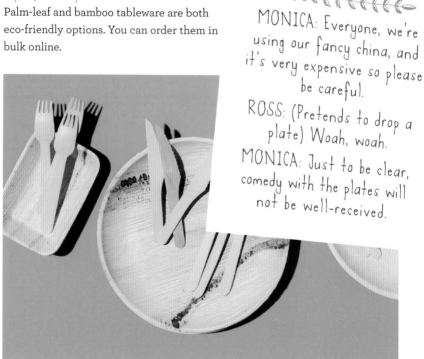

MONICA: Everyone, we're using our fancy china, and it's very expensive so please be careful.

ROSS: (Pretends to drop a plate) Woah, woah.

MONICA: Just to be clear, comedy with the plates will not be well-received.

Serve Buffet Style

A potluck also warrants buffet-style serving. Set up your food and tableware on a side buffet table. If you're making "Happy Friendsgiving" napkin rings and thankful cards (pages 89 and 90), you can place them on the dining room table or on the buffet table with the food. When you're ready to serve dinner, let everyone serve themselves and pick their place to sit at the table. Guests can also clear and dispose of their own dinner plates to pave the way for dessert. Depending on how many desserts you have, you can serve this course either on the side table (once dinner is cleared) or on the main table, along with its own set of plates and forks.

DIY PARTY DECORATIONS

When it comes to your Friendsgiving decorations, DIY is the way to go! Here are some ideas for budget-friendly crowd-pleasers that pay homage to your other favorite group of friends (besides the ones at your party). Plus, you can have a pre-Friendsgiving craft day with your best pals and make everything together.

Food Place Cards

Use cute place cards in the shape of yellow photo frames to display the name of each recipe at your dinner. Mount each place card onto a craft stick or popsicle stick and stick it into the dish. Alternatively, use tent cards or place cards to display the name of each recipe.

Cup Decorations à la Phoebe

When Phoebe is in charge of cups and ice for a party, you better hold on to your cups! Or she just might use them for curtains. Show your friends what you can do with a bunch of cups strung up around your place. Or have a cup-decorating activity sesh!

"Hey, check it out, cup hat, cup banner, cup chandelier, and the thing that started it all, the cup!"
—Phoebe Buffay

Cup ID

Ask your guests to write a pithy alter ego for themselves on a name tag sticker, such as Regina Phalange, Princess Consuela Banana Hammock, or Crap Bag, and stick it on their cups (if you're using disposable cups). Alternatively, create clip-on name badges using name tag labels and clear plastic clip-on holders or lanyards. Don't let anyone drink who isn't wearing a cup ID.

Party Banner

Create a large banner to tie the room together. You can use lots of different icons from the show or stick to one theme, such as coffee cups, umbrellas, or turkeys. Extra points if your turkeys are wearing sunglasses.

SUPPLIES:

Printed pictures

Glue stick

8½ × 11-inch purple copy paper or cardstock

Measuring tape

Yellow yarn or craft twine

Masking tape or painter's tape

Mini wooden clothespins or craft clips

MAKE YOUR BANNER:

1. Print the pictures you want to hang.
2. Glue each one onto a sheet of purple paper and let them dry. (This will give your banner a consistent look.)
3. Measure the space where you plan to hang your banner and cut a long piece of yarn that will drape across the space with enough left over to tape the ends.
4. Secure the string into position on both sides with tape.
5. Using the clothespins, clip each picture onto the banner, spacing them evenly apart.
6. If your banner becomes too heavy, use more tape to secure the yarn midway, or adjust the width between each picture.
7. Stand back and admire your excellent work.

Photo Booth

Stage a photo booth for your guests to commemorate your awesome Friendsgiving. Set up a classy purple fringe backdrop with ample lighting and either a selfie stick or mounted iPad. Then, mount some memorable expressions and icons on cardstock for props. Tape or glue each prop to a stick. Chopsticks work great for props, as we learned when the gang used them to check on Ugly Naked Guy.

PLANNING THE PERFECT POTLUCK MENU

Planning the perfect Friendsgiving potluck menu is a bit like strategizing for the big game.

You want to play to everyone's strengths and show off your best skills. If you're with good friends, you're guaranteed to have a good time no matter what, but still, at the end of the night, you want everyone to go home feeling like, wow, that Friendsgiving was epic! And it all starts with the food.

As the host, you should plan on cooking at least one main dish and one to two side dishes, or one side dish and one dessert. In addition, it's customary as the host to be in charge of beverages, and that means preparing a big-batch cocktail or serving some wine and beer, as well as having a selection of nonalcoholic drinks.

Assuming you're going potluck style, this is when your shareable digital spreadsheet is crucial. As the host, you get dibs on what dishes you're cooking, but it's also smart to make sure your menu is varied. You don't want to have three different kinds of sweet potatoes and two people responsible for bringing pies who are likely to forget (Rachel and Phoebe). So, to avoid a menu catastrophe, follow Monica's lead and do a little damage control before it happens. Assign people to certain menu items, or at least to different meal components (appetizers, sides, desserts). This might sound controlling, but do you want to risk three people showing up with Brussels sprouts?

Chandler, Rachel, and Ross huddle up during a Thanksgiving football game.

* * * * * * * * * * * * *

Spreadsheet Organization

Throw some categories on your spreadsheet that hit all the food groups:

- Meat

- Veggies

- Fruit

- Dessert (yes, this is really a food group when it comes to parties)

Put a couple of "suggestions" (code for *if you're really my friend you'll do this*) at the top of your spreadsheet, such as:

- Sign up to bring a dish and help us work in all the food groups.

- Please bring everything you need to serve your dish.

- Don't bring the same thing as someone else.

- Feel free to also bring a beverage of your choice.

HOW TO HOST LIKE A BOSS ... WITHOUT BEING BOSSY

Monica is the quintessential party planner in that she is incredibly organized, efficient, clean, and a great cook. But being a great *host* takes another set of strengths. It requires patience, flexibility, and people skills. "The One With the Two Parties" is the perfect example. When the gang tries to throw a surprise party for Rachel and both of her parents, who don't get along, show up unexpectedly, the gang separates the guests into two parties—one in Monica's apartment and one in Chandler and Joey's. Monica's hosting style is very strict, while Chandler and Joey's style is loose and fun. As a result, everyone tries to secretly escape Monica's party for Chandler and Joey's. Most people will pick a fun party over a strict party any day, no matter how good the food might be at the latter. Here are a few tips on how to host like a boss ... without being bossy.

Set the Mood for Your Party

Every party (even the fake kind) calls for its own kind of mood. There are tons of suggestions in this book on how to create *Friends*-inspired ambiance, decorations, tablescaping, and more for Friendsgiving.

Joey and Chandler get in on the act to try to help Rachel seduce her crush in "The One With the Fake Party"

Play Good Music

Have your "Ultimate Friendsgiving Playlist" ready (page 108) and know which device and speaker you'll be using. Some of your friends might offer to show off their musical talents. If that happens, be polite, but also be ready to follow up their act with a hit from your playlist.

Monica confronts Phoebe about the "tone" of her music as she plays outside Monica's restaurant.

Be Ready to Roll with Anything

No matter how much you plan, things will always come up. Just roll with it. Remember that everyone is there to have a good time, including you.

Offer a Variety of Games and Activities for Downtime and After Dinner

Board games, card games, memory games, and mental challenge games like Unagi Pictionary and Would You Rather . . . with Friends are perfect for Friendsgiving! (Hint: We've got a whole section of activities for you starting on page 133.) But also be cool if no one wants to play your games.

Chandler and Joey try to figure out how to rescue the chick and duck who are trapped inside their beloved foosball table.

"We're supposed to start having fun in 15 minutes!"

—Monica Geller

Expect the Unexpected Requests

You're going to get some unexpected requests and you don't have to say yes to all of them. For example, a couple of your guests might ask if you can clear out some space for an impromptu dance floor. They want to show everyone "the routine." It's up to you if you want to "pivot" and move the couch.

Ross and Monica perform "The Routine" during a taping of Dick Clark's New Year's Rockin' Eve, hoping to get on television.

Keep the Thermostat Cooler Than Usual

It might be cold outside, but your home shouldn't feel like the tropics like when the heater broke in "The One With Phoebe's Dad" and they ended up having a Christmas summer party . . . or the time the gang actually went to the tropics and learned what it does to Monica's hair. Don't forget that the oven and extra company will cause the temperature to rise. Keep the thermostat at a slightly cooler temperature to keep everyone cool and comfortable.

Humidity gets the best of Monica's hair in "The One in Barbados."

Don't Freak Out if Guests Are Late

You can expect that some people will be later than others. This is par for the course. Do yourself—and them!—a favor and don't lock anyone out like Monica does.

Be Prepared for Some Guests to Linger

Unless you're going to ask everyone to leave by a certain time, which is a little pushy, be prepared for some lingerers. And take it as a compliment. If it starts to get really late, you could try to give people a hint by starting to take out the trash and doing the dishes. And if that doesn't do the trick, put them to work helping you clean up!

The gang says a long, tearful goodbye to each other and the apartment in the final episode of the show.

Remember That You're the Boss!

Don't let anyone rain on your parade (or pour sauce on you) unless you ask for it!

Joey acts out in Monica's restaurant to help her earn the respect of her coworkers.

"Okay people, I want you to take a piece of paper and write down your most embarrassing memory. And I do ask that when you're not using the markers you put the pen caps back on them because they will dry out."
—Monica Geller

THANKSGIVING PANTS AND DRESS-CODE OPTIONS

If you leave the dress code up to interpretation, you might get the unexpected. Don't leave it up to chance. This is the perfect opportunity for a Friendsgiving dress-code theme!

Here are some ways you could go:

Dress like your favorite Friends character.

Dress in a costume from your favorite holiday episode. For the Holiday Armadillo, you'll want to call stores in advance.

Come in your version of Thanksgiving pants (or borrow a friend's maternity pants).

Wear mismatched clothing or as many layers of clothing as possible.

Sport your favorite look from the eighties.

Wear your PJs.

Clothing optional. Keep in mind that this one will be challenging for social media posts.

THE ULTIMATE FRIENDSGIVING PLAYLIST

When you think of *Friends* music, you might find yourself suddenly humming the theme song, "I'll Be There for You," or you might picture Phoebe strumming her guitar (with some questionable lyrics) in Central Perk. Or, you might even be thinking about the time Ross and Rachel surprised us all by busting out a performance of "Baby Got Back" for baby Emma. Whatever your jam, you'll definitely want to cue up some of these hits featured on the show for your Friendsgiving playlist.

First up, here are ten of the most memorable musical moments from the show.

10. "SMELLY CAT MEDLEY"— PHOEBE BUFFAY & THE HAIRBALLS FEATURING THE PRETENDERS

"Smelly Cat" is the most memorable song written by Phoebe Buffay and it has had quite the track record, including a guest-star appearance by Chrissie Hynde, a professional recording, and a jingle for cat litter.

9. "THE LION SLEEPS TONIGHT"— THE TOKENS

It's Marcel's favorite song, which we learn when he hits play on the CD player (remember those?). The song returns in season 2 during the famous Super Bowl episode when the gang visits Marcel on his movie set.

8. "I GO BLIND"—HOOTIE & THE BLOWFISH

Over the course of all ten seasons, the gang goes to one concert and guess what it is? It's Hootie & the Blowfish to celebrate Ross's birthday (though only Ross, Monica, and Chandler actually attend). It makes sense since the band had the best-selling album of 1995 with their debut album, *Cracked Rear View*, which was certified platinum.

7. "IT'S RAINING MEN"—THE WEATHER GIRLS

Monica and Chandler visit Chandler's dad (guest star Kathleen Turner) in Vegas, where he is performing in a show called "4 Queens," and invite him to their wedding. Chandler's dad performs "It's Raining Men" at the end of a heartwarming scene.

6. "LET ME BLOW YA MIND"—EVE FEATURING GWEN STEFANI

Since Monica had a stripper at her bachelorette party and Chandler didn't, Monica does a striptease for him (sort of) to this track from the early 2000s to even things out. It's totally awkward, but the music rocks!

5. "WONDERFUL TONIGHT"—ERIC CLAPTON

After Chandler proposes to Monica, they slow dance as the credits roll and we get chills from Eric Clapton's voice singing, "My darling, you look wonderful tonight."

4. "TAKE A BOW"—MADONNA

Madonna's beautiful and apropos lyrics, "I've always been in love with you," play in the background as Rachel waits excitedly for Ross at the airport, only to find out he's returned with a new girlfriend. Seriously, Ross?

3. "WICKED GAME"—CHRIS ISAAK

This romantic song plays when Ross and Rachel "you know" in the Natural History Museum.

2. "WITH OR WITHOUT YOU"—U2

Ross serenades Rachel over the radio to try to win her back after "the list" fiasco, only to have her call the radio station and ask them to stop playing the song. Our hearts are breaking!

1. "BABY GOT BACK"—SIR MIX-A-LOT

In an episode appropriately titled "The One With Ross's Inappropriate Song," Ross catches us all by surprise when he starts rapping "Baby Got Back" for Emma to her "itty bitty" delight. Rachel resists at first but eventually joins in the fun. I mean, what baby could resist one of the most catchy rap tunes of the nineties?

Here are some more hit songs from the show for your playlist:

✳ ✳ ✳ ✳ ✳ ✳ ✳ ✳ ✳ ✳ ✳ ✳ ✳

"I'll Be There for You" (Theme from *Friends*)—
The Rembrandts

"Top of the World"—
Carpenters

"All By Myself"—
Eric Carmen

"Funky Town"—Lipps

"Space Oddity"—
David Bowie

"Rock and Roll All Nite"—
KISS

"The Fockafeller Skank"—
Fatboy Slim

"Disco Inferno"—
The Trammps

"Love to Love You Baby"—
Donna Summer

"Love Machine"—The Miracles

"You'll Know You Were Loved"—Lou Reed

"Closing Time"—Semisonic

"In My Room"—
Grant Lee Buffalo

"Y.M.C.A."—Village People

Phoebe performs at Central Perk, accompanied by Ross on the bagpipes.

"Angel of the Morning"—
Pretenders

"Girl, You'll Be a Woman Soon"—Neil Diamond

"What's the Frequency, Kenneth?"—R.E.M.

"My Guy"—Mary Wells

"Sky Blue and Black"—
Jackson Browne

"Shiny Happy People"—R.E.M.

"Good Intentions"—
Toad the Wet Sprocket

"Don't Stand So Close to Me"—
The Police

"Big Yellow Taxi"—
Joni Mitchell

"I Will Survive"—
Gloria Gaynor

"Play That Funky Music"—
Wild Cherry

"I Dream of Jeanie"—
Daniel, Fred & Julie

"The Girl of Ipanema"—
Denise King

"Get Down Tonight"—
KC & The Sunshine Band

"Shoebox"—Barenaked Ladies

"We Will Rock You"—Queen

"Celebration"—
Kool & The Gang

"Into Your Arms"—
The Lemonheads

"It's No Good"—
Depeche Mode

"Every Word Means No"—
Smash Mouth

"I Wouldn't Normally Do This
Kind of Thing"—
Robbie Williams

"Careless Whisper"—
George Michael

"Viva Las Vegas"—
Elvis Presley

"London Calling"—The Clash

"Believe"—Cher

"I'm So Excited"—
The Pointer Sisters

"It's Not Unusual"—Tom Jones

"Part-Time Lover"—
Stevie Wonder

"Ride Wit Me"—
Nelly, City Spud

"Walk On"—U2

"Yellow Ledbetter"—Pearl Jam

"A Groovy Kind of Love"—
Phil Collins

"Endless Love"—
Lionel Richie, Diana Ross

"There She Goes"—The La's

"Tupelo Honey"—
Van Morrison

"Looks Like We Made It"—
Barry Manilow

"Delta Dawn"—Tanya Tucker

REHEATING FOOD AND PRIORITIZING OVEN SPACE

Chances are, if your fridge breaks, you're not going to rush to eat everything like Joey Tribbiani. When it comes to a potluck, it's best to plan on serving dishes at room temperature. Why? Your fridge and oven can only hold so much and you'll be juggling a lot at once. Plus, you don't want everyone hanging out in your kitchen.

How to properly reheat food at your Friendsgiving:

Tip: Be sure to allow time for the oven to preheat.

MEAT DISHES:
Reheat meat dishes in the oven at 350°F for 20 to 30 minutes. Make sure there is a little liquid in the pan, such as 1 cup of warm water or stock (so the meat doesn't toughen up), and avoid overcooking.

VEGETABLE SIDE DISHES:
Reheat vegetables in a 350°F oven for 15 to 20 minutes.

USING A MICROWAVE:
The microwave is useful for smaller sides that don't need to be crisped, such as mashed potatoes and yams. Just remember that microwaves cook things unevenly, so you need to reheat in short increments of time, stir, and heat again. Avoid using the microwave to reheat meats as it will make them rubbery.

"The fridge broke, so I had to eat everything."
—Joey Tribbiani

HOW TO PRIORITIZE WHAT TO REHEAT:

It's your oven, your call! That being said, take a look at your spreadsheet before the big day and try to get a sense of what will need reheating. If you're worried about making it all fit in your oven and your timeframe, don't be afraid to ask your friends if they wouldn't mind if you serve their dishes at room temperature.

MONICA'S TOWELS AND OTHER HOUSEHOLD ESSENTIALS

When you're entertaining and it comes to basic household necessities, you'll want to have more than a "pla." So while this may sound like common sense, if you don't want to run into an awkward situation, do yourself a favor and make sure your supplies are stocked.

Towels

Monica has eleven categories of towels. You don't need quite that many, but you should put some nice hand towels in the guest bathroom and have paper towels on hand for cleanups.

ROSS: Monica categorizes her towels. How many categories are there?

JOEY: Everyday use.

CHANDLER: Fancy.

JOEY: Guest.

CHANDLER: Fancy guest.

Toilet Paper

There will be no toilet paper–folding lessons in this book. But it is recommended you have an ample supply of TP and that you make sure extra rolls are readily accessible for guests.

"I want to show you how to fold the toilet paper into a point."

—Monica Geller

Cleaning Agents and Trash Bags

You certainly don't need to make your own cleaning sprays like Monica, but you will want to have some good cleaning agents available to your guests during the party and for yourself for post-party cleanup:

- Hand soap (preferably in a nice pump dispenser) for the bathroom

- Stain remover

- Cleaning sprays (including carpet/upholstery cleaner)

- Magic Erasers

- Heavy-duty trash bags

Additional Items for the Bathroom

What happens in the bathroom should absolutely stay in the bathroom, but there was that one time that Joey emerged from Monica's bathroom with a newspaper and no one had any idea how long he had been in there or that he had been in there at all, for that matter. So, on that note, here are a few additional suggested supplies to have in the bathroom:

MONICA: Do you have a plan?
PHOEBE: I don't even have a "pla."

- A nice lotion that goes with your hand soap

- Some Poo-Pourri spray or a book of matches

- Basic toiletries that guests might appreciate, such as feminine products, mouthwash, dental floss, and paper rinsing cups. They can be stored in a nice basket on the counter or in a vanity cabinet.

DINNERTIME AND LATECOMERS

When you're hosting a dinner party, it's best to count backwards to figure out your start time and serving time. Dinner should be planned for at least one hour to an hour and a half later than the start time on the invitation. Before dinner you'll be hosting a warm-up hour with cocktails and hors d'oeuvres. Let's say you'd like to serve dinner at 7:00 p.m. and have your warm-up time from 6:00 to 7:00 p.m. But what happens when guests show up late? You might as well figure most of your guests will be trickling in during the first half hour—that's pretty standard. So, have a game plan with times in mind while also allowing for a bit of wiggle room. For example:

6:00–6:30 P.M.
Greet guests, have cocktails and appetizers

6:30–7:00 P.M.
Do a scan of the room; if most guests are there, turn on the oven to get ready to reheat food; if you're still waiting for a number of guests, wait another 15 minutes.

If anyone shows up once you've started dinner, they will just need to catch up to the rest of the party. You can be a good host without letting other people's timeliness (or lack thereof) stress you out.

7:00–7:15 P.M.
Heat dishes in the oven

7:15 / 7:20 P.M.
Serve dinner

MONICA: I can't believe this. They're an hour late and they're just standing out there talking . . .
CHANDLER: Ross's shirt is torn.
MONICA: They're late and they're sloppy.

Joey gets his head stuck in Monica's door after being late for Thanksgiving dinner.

HOW TO GIVE A FRIENDSGIVING TOAST

We've learned a lot about giving speeches from the gang's celebrations over a decade, whether for a wedding, anniversary, or holiday. Here are some of the best lessons we've learned:

If you're going to say just a few words, make sure it's not in gibberish.

"We are gathered here today on this joyous occasion to celebrate the special love that Monica and Chandler share. . . . And the love that they give and have is shared and received. And through this having and giving and sharing and receiving, we too can share and love and have . . . and receive."
—Joey Tribbiani

"I'd like to toast Ross and Emily. Of course my big toast will be tomorrow at the wedding, so this is my little toast or Melba toast, if you will. . . . I'm sure we're all very excited that Ross and Emily are getting married in Montgomery Hall. I mean to think my friend getting married in Monty Hall. Oh come on—Monty Hall, Let's Make a Deal? Come on, you people!"
—Chandler Bing

Try your best not to bomb, but if you do, do it with gusto.

Giving a toast with the goal of eliciting an emotional response is probably not the best idea.

"When I look around this room, I'm saddened by the thought of those who could not be with us. Nanna, my beloved grandmother, who would so wanna be here, but she can't, because she's dead. As is our dog, Chi-Chi. I mean, look how cute she is . . . was."
—Monica Geller

"I'll always be their friend . . . their friend who can speak in many dialects and has training in stage combat and is willing to do partial nudity. Oh! To the happy couple!"
—Joey Tribbiani

Trying to impress the audience with your acting résumé is a definite no-no.

So just what *should* go into a Friendsgiving toast?

Here are a few suggestions:

- It should make sense.

- It should be relevant to the people you're toasting.

- It should be memorable and meaningful without going overboard.

- It should not be used to try to force emotion out of the recipients.

- If it works for your party, make it a group toast and let the rest of your friends join in!

Come to think of it, if you look at the gang's toast from their very first Thanksgiving episode, it's pretty close to perfect.

CHANDLER: All right, I'd like to propose a toast. A little toast here. Ding, ding! I know this isn't exactly the Thanksgiving all of you planned but for me, this has been really great, you know. I think because it didn't involve divorce or projectile vomiting. Anyway, I was just thinking if you'd gone to Vail, or if you guys had been with your family, or if you didn't have syphilis and stuff, we wouldn't be all together. So, I guess what I'm trying to say is that I'm very thankful that all of your Thanksgivings sucked.

PHOEBE: That's so sweet!

RACHEL: Thank you.

ROSS: And hey, here's to a lousy Christmas!

RACHEL: And a crappy New Year!

HOW TO LOOK GREAT
IN GROUP PHOTOS
AND RE-CREATE EPIC CAST SHOTS

Have you wondered how the gang always looks so amazing in group photos? Is it because they are all incredibly photogenic? Because they have talented photographers? Because they know how to nail the best poses? Yes. Yes. And yes. But you can work your next group photo shoot like a pro too with just a few tips and tricks.

Lighting

Daytime light is completely different than nighttime light. If you're hosting a dinner party, you'll be contending with indoor, low light where there can be a lot of shadows and contrast. You need to bring more light balance to your shots. A portable ring light is a great tool to help compensate for lighting issues on a smartphone, as is a DSLR with the right settings and an external flash. It also helps to find out right away which of your buddies have the best cameras for low-light photography. Some of the newer smartphones have specific settings for low light. DSLR cameras will also have lots of settings and good flashes. Those are the cameras you should use for big group shots.

Edit Photos with a Smartphone Editing App

Take advantage of some cool filters and face editing apps to stylize your photos. Just be careful not to overdo it on the face editing. You still want to look like you!

Stabilize Shots with a Tripod with a Remote Control

Why should you get a good tripod with a remote control? Because a tripod stabilizes your smartphone even more than a selfie stick. And if you have a remote control, you can get really professional with your photos.

Invest in a Selfie Stick

Your arm can only extend so far. A selfie stick makes it easier to capture all different angles and is useful for both selfies and group shots. It also helps to stabilize your shots. And your arm won't get tired!

Save the "Turkey Neck" for Dinnertime

Don't take photos with the camera below eye level. This will only result in bizarre chin-neck proportions. Keeping the lens above a subject's head elongates and flatters the neck. You can also push your chin slightly forward in darker light to avoid harsh shadows on your chin and neck.

Wear a Little Extra Makeup

Play up your features with a little more makeup and contouring whenever you'll be in nighttime or darker lighting.

Orchestrate the Shots

Now that you've got some moves and techniques down, get your cameras, props, and smiles ready to re-create some of the most iconic cast photography! These can all be orchestrated with a little creative direction and a tripod or a selfie stick.

The One In the Bathtub

Make sure your tub is pristinely clean and dry in advance. Add some rubber duckies and bubble blowing into your photo.

The One With the Milkshakes

Times have changed and non-reusable straws are out. But you can still have milkshakes, ice-cream sundaes, and grab a spoon! And then you can play an actual game of "Grab a Spoon" (page 156).

The One With the Sexy Clock Poses

If you don't have a conveniently placed standing clock or staircase landing to hang on to, just gather around a wall clock and pose.

The One On the Staircase

Um . . . this is probably going to be an awkward photo no matter what, so give it your best shot—(literally). Have one person hold a selfie stick in the air above everyone's faces to capture the pic. Just have fun with it!

The One Where Everyone Hugs

Pair up and show your friends how much they mean to you.

The One Where They Strut Down the Street

Set up a tripod and camera timer. Then, strut your stuff with your friends down the street (a.k.a. your hallway), in whichever Friendsgiving dress code you chose (see "Thanksgiving Pants and Dress-Code Options," page 104).

RUMOR CONTROL
WHEN FRIENDS AREN'T GETTING ALONG

Hopefully, there won't be any physical fighting at your party. But the fact is, no matter how carefully you plan out your guest list, you may run into a situation where a couple of guests just aren't getting along. Case in point: when Monica invites Will (guest star Brad Pitt), an old friend from high school, for Thanksgiving dinner. Little does she realize that he still harbors resentment toward Rachel for being mean to him all those years ago.

Before you even send your invitations, it's wise to think about whether there will be good chemistry among everyone invited. But you have no control over what might be going on personally between other people.

Should you run into a situation where there are bad feelings between two of your guests, don't let it cramp your style. Here are a few tips on how to handle conflict:

Stay Neutral

Being the host is like being captain of a team. You don't want to take sides against your own teammates or play referee.

Set Boundaries

If there's too much tension, designate a friend to try to separate the guests in opposite sides of the room, or if necessary, encourage them to go into another room to talk things out privately.

Joey: Hey now . . . hey . . . now! And I'm bleeding.

Phoebe: Oh, oh, wow, and I'm a vegetarian.

Phoebe takes stage fighting one step too far when she lands a real punch to Joey's nose.

Create a Diversion

Suggest a fun activity or pump up your "Ultimate Friendsgiving Playlist" (page 108).

Whatever Happens, Keep the Party Going

Your role as the host is to make everyone feel comfortable and show them a good time.

WILL: We started a rumor.

RACHEL: What rumor?

PHOEBE: Oh come on, Will, just take off your shirt and tell us.

RACHEL: Ross!

ROSS: It's no big deal. We said . . . the rumor was that you had both male and female reproductive parts.

WILL: That's right. We said your parents flipped a coin and decided to raise you as a girl but you still had a hint of a penis.

DOGGY BAGS
AND WHAT TO DO WITH LEFTOVERS

When you work really hard on a dish, it's a shame to see the leftovers go to waste. But you can't possibly fit everyone's leftovers in your refrigerator or eat them all. Here are some ways to avoid wasting all that great food.

Have Some "Doggy Bags" Ready for Guests

Purchase some inexpensive containers, zipper bags, foil, and plastic wrap. You can get all of these items at a dollar store. Encourage your friends to put together a "doggy bag" for themselves before they leave.

Repurpose Leftovers into Other Meals

The Moist Maker just might go down as the most famous use of turkey leftovers in history—at least television history. If you have leftover turkey, make your own Moist Maker (page 58). Extra meat and veggies can usually be repurposed into other dishes over the next couple of days, such as soups, salads, and sides.

Freeze Your Favorites for the Future

Many dishes can be frozen for two to three months and will stay good as long as they are kept in freezer-safe containers or freezer bags.

ROSS: You ate my sandwich?
DR. LEDBETTER: It was a simple mistake. It could happen to anyone.
ROSS: Oh, oh, really? Did you confuse your own turkey sandwich with a Moist Maker?

Don't Forget to Label

Make sure to label each item you store in the freezer with its date and name. Dates will remind you to use what you have before it starts getting freezer burn. Names will remind you what they actually are. You wouldn't want someone to accidentally "drink the fat" like Joey. If you bring your leftovers to work, especially the Moist Maker, make sure to label everything with your name. No need to go overboard, though; you don't want your coworkers calling you "mental" like Ross.

DR. LEDBETTER: No, I . . .

ROSS: Do you perhaps remember seeing a note on top of IT?

DR. LEDBETTER: There may have been a joke or a limerick of some kind.

ROSS: That said it was MY sandwich.

DR. LEDBETTER: Now, now calm down. Come look in my office. Some of it may still be in the trash.

ROSS: What?

DR. LEDBETTER: Well, it was quite large. I had to throw most of it away.

ROSS: You-you-you threw my sandwich away? MY sandwich? MY SANDWICH?

TIPS FOR CLEANING UP

Ah, if only cleaning up was hot . . . it's not. But there is an order to it, and hopefully with a little foresight and planning you can avoid feeling like a hot mess after your party is over.

Don't Save All the Cleanup Until the End

You can and should tackle smaller cleanup tasks during the party. Clear away each course after it's done. Don't let it stress you out or keep you from enjoying the party, but it's the right etiquette to clear after each course once everyone is done to make room for the next one.

Label Bins for Trash and Recycling

Make sure guests know where the bins are and what goes where. You can use a label maker like Monica or make some cute signs for them. This will also hopefully encourage your guests to take the liberty of doing some of the cleanup themselves.

Know Where Your Cleaning Supplies Are and Make Sure They're Stocked

Something as simple as putting everything you might need into a bucket in advance could be a welcome relief when you're exhausted and looking for your carpet cleaner. Definitely make sure to have an ample supply of heavy-duty trash bags on hand.

Plan for Dirty Dishes and Disposable Dinnerware

Make sure your dishwasher is empty before your party starts. If you're using real dishes, stack them in the sink until you get a chance to load them into the dishwasher between courses. If you're using disposable dinnerware, direct your guests to the recycling and trash.

Have Storage Containers Clean and Ready

Large storage containers and gallon-size zipper bags are ideal for storing your own leftover food and packing up doggy bags for guests. (See "Doggy Bags and What to Do with Leftovers," page 128.")

Have a Plan for Your Tablecloths

If disposable, toss 'em! If machine washable, clear everything off and throw them in the laundry room or straight into the washing machine.

Always Do the Floor Last

Everything winds up on the floor. Do everything else first. Then sweep and vacuum. Note that you do not need to vacuum your vacuum like Monica does.

Be Grateful if Your Guests Offer to Help

If your friends offer to pitch in and you feel comfortable with it, take them up on it. Obviously, you're not going to ask them to get on their hands and knees and scrub the floor, but every extra set of hands is helpful. Just be grateful even if they don't put things exactly where they go. You can fix it later—just like Monica does after Chandler tries to impress her by cleaning her apartment and puts everything in the wrong place.

MONICA: You should go to the game, it's okay, I want you to.

CHANDLER: Really? You gonna be okay?

MONICA: Yeah, I'll be fine. Yeah, maybe, I'll stay here and practice the art of seduction.

CHANDLER: You're gonna put sweats on and clean, aren't you?

MONICA: It's gonna be so hot!

The gang takes a break from a heated game of football during Thanksgiving in "The One With the Football."

RACHEL: Oh Monica, that was the best Thanksgiving dinner ever. It was so good. I think you killed us.

ROSS: Couldn't possibly eat another bite.

JOEY: I need something sweet.

PHOEBE: Does anyone wanna watch TV? Monica, your remote doesn't work.

MONICA: Phoebe, you have to lift it and point.

PHOEBE: Oh. Oh forget it.

PART THREE

ACTIVITIES

AT THIS POINT IN YOUR EVENT, you're likely coming up on what I like to call the post-meal hangover. You went all out and planned the perfect *Friends*-styled Friendsgiving—YAAAS! Good for you! From the ambiance to the food to your gracious hosting, it couldn't have gone better. So maybe now everyone's feeling a little full, a little sleepy, and even clicking the remote control seems like too much work. But you want to keep the party going! So what do you do? It's time to bring out the house party games! Because surprise, surprise, you have planned for this moment well in advance and, little do your guests know, your *Friends*-themed activity-planning skills are off the hook—as is your knowledge of dinosaurs. But we'll get to that in a minute.

⊙ A FRIENDS ⊙
DRINKING GAME

This game can be played with or without alcohol. The fun is in taking a sip of your beverage of choice whenever your *Friends* character does or says something described in the rules below. Drinks can be as appealing or unappealing as you want. For example, you could serve delicious milkshakes so everyone is cheering their characters on until they can take the next sip. Or, you could go in a totally different direction and force everyone to drink water with a splash of olive juice. Be prepared for some groans and less cheering. Either way, the game will be a hit!

SUPPLIES:
Scratch paper

A *Friends* episode

Beverage of choice for
   each player

PREP:
Write down each of the six main
characters' names on six slips of paper:
Rachel, Ross, Monica, Chandler, Phoebe, and Joey.

Rachel describes her first kiss with Ross over drinks with the girls.

HOW TO PLAY:
Each guest picks a slip of paper to reveal his/her character identity. If you have more than six guests, pair up or triple up. If you have fewer than six, you can either have more than one identity (smaller sips recommended) or leave some characters out. Next, cue up a *Friends* episode, make sure everyone's cups are full, and let the game commence!

Monica drinks each time:

- She says "I know!"
- She says something bossy.
- She cooks or cleans.
- Someone makes a joke about when she was overweight.

Chandler drinks each time:

- He says something sarcastic.
- He uses the word "BE" in a sentence with emphasis.
- He says something self-deprecating.
- He makes a reference to his dad or his childhood.

Rachel drinks each time:

- She says "Noo!"
- She calls someone "honey."
- She makes fun of Ross.
- She talks about someone she has a crush on.

Ross drinks each time:

- He talks about dinosaurs or his job.
- The subject of his divorces comes up.
- He talks about Rachel.
- He says "Hi" or makes a sad face.

Phoebe drinks each time:

- She sings.
- She mentions the days when she lived on the street or her mother's suicide.
- She says something ditzy.
- She refers to being a vegetarian.

Joey drinks each time:

- He talks about food.
- He rehearses lines or refers to Dr. Drake Ramoray.
- He crushes on a woman.
- He says "How you doin'?"

THE THANKFUL GAME

Of course, to play the thankful game, you could go around in a circle and have everyone say what they're thankful for, but you're far more creative than that. In fact, if you're anything like Monica and crave more structure in your gaming, take it to the next level with a game board prepared in advance.

SUPPLIES:

A large piece of cardboard, recycled box, or whiteboard

A bag of Skittles or M&Ms

A marker

Elmer's glue or tape

PREP:

1. Hang the game board, and grab your bag of Skittles or M&Ms.
2. On your board, write a list of five things one can be thankful for.
3. Glue or tape a different colored piece of candy beside each item on the list.

For example, your board might say something like this:

THE THANKFUL GAME
Share a memory you're thankful for. (red skittle)
Name a person you're thankful for. (orange skittle)
Share a skill you're thankful for. (yellow skittle)
Name a food you're thankful for. (green skittle)
Share an experience you're thankful for. (purple skittle)

thank you!

RACHEL: We should play that game where everyone says one thing that they're thankful for.

JOEY: I am thankful for this beautiful fall we've been having . . . the other day I was at the bus stop and this lovely fall breeze just came in out of nowhere and blew this chick's skirt right up.

HOW TO PLAY:

Place the rest of the candy in a bowl. Take turns picking one piece at a time and, using the board as a color guide, name what you are most thankful for.

MEMORY WITH FRIENDS

You don't have to be as organized as Monica to play this game, but you do need a little prep in advance. This activity is a super-fun way to relive past memories with your friends while making new ones.

SUPPLIES:

Printed photos

A table

PREP:

1. Once you've confirmed your guest list, scroll through your phone, social media accounts, or wherever your favorite photos are stored.
2. Select anywhere from twenty-five to fifty photos starring you and your guests. The more photos you use, the bigger your game board will be.
3. Print two 4 × 6-inch copies of each photo.

HOW TO PLAY:

1. Decide if you'll each play individually or split into teams of two. Teams work well if you have a larger group.
2. Mix up the photos.
3. Lay all the photos facedown on a table.

4. Each player (or team) takes a turn and flips over two photos at a time. If they are a match, the player keeps them as a pair and goes again. If they are not a match, the player turns them back over and the next player goes.

5. Once all the photos have been matched, players count up their pairs and the player with the highest number of pairs wins the game.

"Okay, I've broken them down into categories. Okay, we have uh, we got holidays, birthdays, candids, y'know . . . and then what I've done is I've cross-referenced them by subject. Right? So if you're looking up, oh let's say birthdays and dogs, you get Photo 152. See?"

—Monica Geller

DINOSAUR EGG HUNT

Ross takes his dinosaur facts very seriously. How much do you and your friends know about these prehistoric creatures? Test your paleontology and detective skills with a dinosaur egg hunt and name challenge.

SUPPLIES:

A set of plastic Easter eggs

A set of mini dinosaur figures (small enough to fit inside the eggs)

A printed chart of the most common dinosaur names
and corresponding photos, such as: Tyrannosaurus rex,
Stegosaurus, Pterodactyl, Triceratops, Brontosaurus,
Diplodocus, Parasaurolophus, Ankylosaurus, and
Spinosaurus.

PREP:

1. Purchase a set of plastic Easter eggs and a set of mini dinosaur figures small enough to fit inside the eggs. Both can be purchased online and you may also be able to find prefilled eggs with dino toys already inside.
2. Next, place a dino toy inside each egg (if they aren't prefilled).
3. Hide the eggs around your entertaining space. The more you can hide, the more fun it will be.
4. Post the chart on your wall that identifies the most common dinosaur names and pictures.
5. Decide in advance if you want to award prizes
   and, if so, purchase those as well.

ROSS: I have sex with dinosaurs?

CHANDLER: I believe I read that somewhere.

ROSS: Not only is it not funny, it's physically impossible. Depending on the species I'd have to have a six foot long . . . it's not funny!

HOW TO PLAY:

1. On your mark, get set, go! See who can gather the most dinosaur eggs. Seekers have to hold all of their eggs at once without using any carrying tools and without dropping them.

2. Once all the eggs have been found, count them up to see who found the most eggs. Then, test everyone's knowledge by asking them to identify the dinosaurs.

3. Prizes can be awarded to whoever finds the most eggs and whoever guesses the most dinosaur names correctly.

4. Then, it's time to play with your dinosaurs. Watch out for the Tyrannosaurus rex. He might still be hungry.

PIN THE TAIL ON UGLY NAKED GUY

What could BE more fun after a good meal and some drinks than going old school with a round of "Pin the Tail on Ugly Naked Guy"? Here's the catch—you pick the photo (or draw a picture) and decide where the "tail" goes. Oh and by the way, since we never actually see the face of Ugly Naked Guy, feel free to make him look as ugly or as naked as you want.

SUPPLIES:

Large printed photo of "Ugly Naked Guy" (suggested size 11 × 17 inches)

Paper cut into strips for each player to use as a "tail." Write the player's name on each strip to keep track of whose is whose, and stick a piece of tape on one end.

Scotch tape or masking tape

A red marker

A scarf to use as a blindfold

PREP:

1. Hang up your portrait of Ugly Naked Guy so it's about eye level.

2. Designate a spot to pin the tail. Mark it with a red *X*.

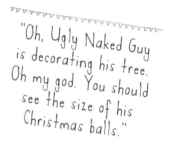

"Oh, Ugly Naked Guy is decorating his tree. Oh my god. You should see the size of his Christmas balls."

—Phoebe Buffay

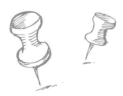

The gang uses a giant stick made out of chopsticks to check the vitals on Ugly Naked Guy.

HOW TO PLAY:

One at a time, blindfold each player and spin him/her around three times. Let the player walk forward and try to "pin" the tail on the *X*. The player with the tail closest to the *X* wins. Recommended after playing "A *Friends* Drinking Game" (see page 134) for obvious reasons.

STICKER STALK YOUR FRIENDS

Remember when Phoebe fell for her twin sister's stalker? Now you can play stalker with your friends . . . with stickers! There's just one catch—you must start the game and explain the rules at the beginning of the party. By the end of the evening, you just might find out who's the stealthiest sticker stalker among all your friends!

SUPPLIES:

Printable sticker labels (name tag and address labels work great)

A printer

A marker

PREP:

Using the fifteen phrases or expressions on the next page (or your own faves), type up a sheet of labels for each guest. Play with different font styles and sizes for each sticker. This works nicely so you can let guests tear stickers into smaller pieces if they want, so long as they get the whole expression to appear on their target. Most importantly, after you create your template, be sure to number each guest's sheet of stickers so they can be tracked back to that person. For example, guest #1 will have a "1" on each sticker, guest #2 will have a "2," etc. It's easiest if you create the same template for each guest, then use a marker to handwrite the numbers on each sheet.

PHRASES:

Unagi

Pivot

Regina Phalange

I'd rather be watching *Friends*

We were on a break!

Love, laughter, and *Friends*

Central Perk

Joey doesn't share food

He's her lobster

Marcel the monkey

How you doin'?

Smelly Cat

Crap bag

Susie Underpants

Grab a spoon

HOW TO PLAY:

Give each guest a sheet of numbered stickers upon arrival and explain the rules of the game. The goal is to try to place as many stickers as possible on other guests throughout the party without them noticing as a sticker is put on them.. If you get caught placing a sticker, then you have to wear it yourself. Whoever has placed the most stickers from their sheet on *other* people by the end of the party wins. And if no one wins, well, then just enjoy some good laughs with a sticker party!

HOW WELL DO YOU KNOW YOUR FRIENDS?

When the girls play this game against the guys, they bet their apartment . . . and lose! Your stakes don't have to be quite that high. Test your friends' knowledge about each other and let the shenanigans that ensue be their own reward.

SUPPLIES:
Game board (poster board or whiteboard)

4 index cards per player

Tape

Writing utensils

A coin

PREP:
Count up the number of players and distribute four index cards to each player. Write the following categories on one side of each set of cards: Fears and Pet Peeves, Literature, It's All Relative, and Ancient History. (Feel free to change the categories.) When ready to play, pass a set of cards to each player and ask them to write a question and answer for each category on the other side of the card. Then, they should pass all the cards back to the host, who will tape them to each category on the board. Divide into two teams.

HOW TO PLAY:
Each team has to answer questions about opposing teammates. The first team to answer ten questions correctly wins. Do a coin toss to see which team will go first. Make sure someone actually calls heads or tails (wink, wink).

GAME CATEGORIES AND EXAMPLES:

Use these categories as your guide to create your board or feel free to swap in different ones.

Fears and Pet Peeves

Question: What is Monica's biggest pet peeve?
Answer: Animals dressed as humans

Ancient History

Question: What was Monica's nickname when she was a field hockey goalie?
Answer: Big Fat Goalie

It's All Relative

Question: What is the name of Monica and Ross's grandmother?
Answer: Althea

Literature

Question: What name appears on the *TV Guide* that comes to Chandler and Joey's apartment?
Answer: Ms. Chanandler Bong

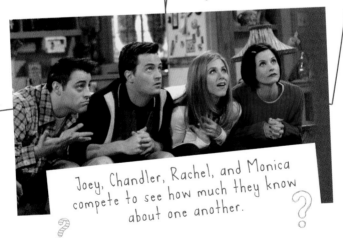

Joey, Chandler, Rachel, and Monica compete to see how much they know about one another.

If you run into a tie, you can play an optional lightning round. Each team gets thirty seconds to answer as many questions as they can. The team that answers the most questions correctly wins.

SCENE: GUESS WHICH FRIENDS CHARACTER I AM

You don't need a headshot to be an actor like Joey. Show your friends what kind of acting chops you have by making them guess which *Friends* character you're playing.

SUPPLIES:
Index cards or scratch paper torn into small pieces
A writing utensil

PREP:
In advance, write the name of each major character from the show on an index card, using the list on the next page as your guide.

HOW TO PLAY:
Divide into two teams. One player from each team takes a turn picking a card. Set a timer on a smartphone for one minute. The player gets sixty seconds to act the part of the character and must stay "in character" the whole time. The player is allowed to speak and use lines from the show and also refer to other characters. However, the player is not allowed to say the character's name. The player's own team has to guess which character he/she is playing within the time limit. This could be the character's relationship to one of the six friends or their actual name. Bonus points if they get the name of the character correct. For example, let's say a player is acting as Phoebe's brother's wife. If the player's team were to guess "Phoebe's brother's wife," they would be correct. If they were to also mention that her name is Alice, they would get an extra point. And if anyone picks the card with Ugly Naked Guy, good luck!

Joey explains the art of "padding" your acting résumé.

* * * * * * * * * * * * *

CHARACTER LIST:

- Monica Geller
- Rachel Green
- Phoebe Buffay
- Chandler Bing
- Ross Geller
- Joey Tribbiani
- Janice, Chandler's ex-girlfriend
- Gunther, manager of Central Perk
- Judy Geller, Monica and Ross's mom
- Jack Geller, Monica and Ross's dad
- Frank, Phoebe's brother
- Alice, Phoebe's brother's wife

- Ursula, Phoebe's twin sister
- Mike, Phoebe's husband
- Amy, Rachel's sister
- Jill, Rachel's sister
- Carol, Ross's ex-wife
- Ben, Ross's son
- Emma, Rachel and Ross's baby
- Richard, Monica's ex-boyfriend
- Julie, Ross's ex-girlfriend with whom he returns from China
- Emily, Ross's British ex-wife
- The Holiday Armadillo
- Ugly Naked Guy

CUP DECORATING

Cup decorating is a perfect activity to do with friends during your warm-up hour or anytime they want to get artsy during the party. It's also a nice ice-breaker if any of your guests are just getting to know each other. For the cups themselves, you have lots of options. You can use large plastic cups like Phoebe used. You can get a little fancier and use plastic, stemless wineglasses. Both are great options for drinking Monica's Tiki Death Punch (page 23) or sipping on wine. Or, if you want to splurge and go a different route altogether, you can purchase white mugs—perfect for Mulled Apple Cider (page 24). Mug decorating tip: To set the Sharpie marker writing permanently, bake the mugs in the oven. Place the mugs into a cool oven, then turn the heat to 350°F and bake for 30 minutes. Leave the mug in the oven until it cools completely so there won't be any cracks.

SUPPLIES:

A set of cups of your choice

Glue

Tape

Colored markers (Sharpies have a good point and can be used to write on everything)

Name tag stickers so guests can write clever names for themselves

Stick-on jewels (glitter is way too messy)

Small pom-poms (very cute if you're up for also using glue)

Stick-on googly eyes (so fun!)

Feathers (ooh la la!)

Any other craft supplies you like

PHOEBE: Looks like you took care of everything. Thanks a lot, co-host.
MONICA: I didn't take care of everything. There's plenty of things for you to do.
PHOEBE: Oh yeah, like what?
MONICA: Cups!
PHOEBE: Cups? You're giving me cups?
MONICA: And ice.
PHOEBE: Cups and ice. Oh I get to be in charge of cups and ice. Alright, fine, okay, I WILL be in charge of cups and ice.

PREP:

Set up an arts and crafts table with your cups and supplies. Use a disposable purple tablecloth (in honor of Monica's walls) as an art mat.

HOW TO PLAY:

Invite your guests to the cup-decorating station upon their arrival. Encourage your friends to really get in there and bedazzle and bling out their cups. And remind them to personalize their cups with their cup IDs (see "DIY Party Decorations," page 94)!

CONVERSATION CARDS

Spread a little wit and sarcasm at your party with these thirty one-liners from the gang about food and Thanksgiving.

SUPPLIES:

Index cards or printer paper (if using printer paper, make four cards per sheet)

A writing utensil or printer

Basket (optional)

PREP:

Write or print one of the lines from the following pages on each index card or printer paper. Place the cards in a stack or basket.

HOW TO PLAY:

Ask guests to take a card from the stack upon their arrival and not to show their card to anyone. Each player has to work the line into conversation to another guest at some point during the party and then wait for the person to guess which character from the show said the line. If the guesser gets it wrong, doesn't know, or fails to notice it's a line (gasp), then the player has to move on to someone else at the party until the origin of the line is guessed correctly. These zingers are fun to use anytime during the party, but especially when your friends are least expecting it. Once the line is guessed correctly, players can choose to grab another card. If you want to make it competitive, see how many cards players can work into conversation, then count them up at the end to find a winner.

LINES:

1. "Cheese. It's milk that you chew." (Chandler)
2. "Once Monica was sent to her room without dinner so she ate the macaroni off a jewelry box she'd made." (Ross)

Just because we don't eat the meat doesn't mean we don't like to play with the carcass.

Joey gets his head stuck in a turkey while trying to scare Chandler.

3. "Oh, oh sweet lord! This is what evil must taste like." (Phoebe)

4. "Someone ate the only good thing in my life." (Ross)

5. "I wasn't supposed to put beef in the trifle." (Rachel)

6. "Look, you're a really nice person . . . ham stealing and adultery aside." (Chandler)

7. "Well, the fridge broke, so I had to eat everything." (Joey)

8. "Crackers. Because your cheese needs a buddy." (Chandler)

9. "I put three lasagnas in your freezer." (Monica)

10. "What's not to like? Custard: good! Jam: good! Meat: goooood!" (Joey)

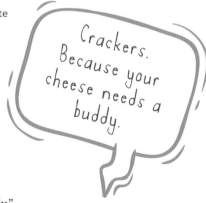

Crackers. Because your cheese needs a buddy.

11. "I'm full, and yet I know if I stop eating this, I'll regret it." (Chandler)

12. "I gotta ask, the girl from the Xerox place buck naked or a big tub of jam?" (Chandler)

13. "That's a great story. Can I eat it?" (Joey)

What, I can't have a mimosa with breakfast? I'm on vacation!

14. "Okay, guys, I have exactly twenty-eight minutes before I have to baste again." (Monica)

15. "Food. Give me." (Joey)

16. "It wouldn't be Thanksgiving without a little emotional scarring." (Ross)

17. "No matter what happens, we still get cake, right?" (Joey)

18. "They've ruined cranberry day!" (Chandler)

19. "You can't have Thanksgiving without turkey. That's like Fourth of July without apple pie or Friday with no two pizzas." (Joey)

20. "It's Thanksgiving and we should not want to be together, together!" (Rachel)

21. "That turkey has to feed twenty people at my parents' house and they're not going to eat it off your head!" (Monica)

22. "Set another place for Thanksgiving. My entire family thinks I have VD." (Joey)

23. "Don't you put words in people's mouths. You put turkey in people's mouths." (Joey)

24. "Some people have said it's 'little drops of heaven.' But whatever." (Monica)

25. "Hummus, I got the hummus!" (Phoebe)

26. "Just cut me a little sliver. A little bigger. Little bigger. What, are you afraid you're going to run out, cut me a real piece!" (Joey)

27. "What, I can't have a mimosa with breakfast? I'm on vacation!" (Phoebe)

28. "Just because we don't eat the meat doesn't mean we don't like to play with the carcass." (Phoebe)

29. "I could be a vegetarian. There's no meat in beer, right?" (Joey)

30. "But to me that is not scary 'cause I stay away from dairy." (Phoebe)

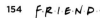

TWO TRUTHS AND A LIE ... ABOUT YOUR FRIENDS

This is a good ice-breaker to play in a circle. And that is *not* a lie.

SUPPLIES:

Index cards or scratch paper for each player

Writing utensil for each player

HOW TO PLAY:

Ask each guest to come up with three statements about themselves, two that are true and one that is a lie. Guests may choose to write them down so they don't forget, or they can commit them to memory. Go around in a circle, letting one player go at a time. The player to the left has to guess which statement is the lie. If the player guesses correctly, then that player gets to state two new truths and a lie for the next person. However, if the player guesses incorrectly, that player skips a turn and the player making the statement moves on to the next player.

Rachel and Joey discover they are both late to Monica's Thanksgiving dinner and try to come up with a good lie.

GRAB A SPOON

Get ready to grab a spoon! But first, you'll need to collect four of a kind. There are many variations of this card game, which you may know as Spoons or Pig. It's fun to play as a speed game with a large group of friends during or after dessert. Just make sure you have enough spoons for eating and playing.

SUPPLIES:

A deck of cards (jokers removed). If you have more than six players, use two decks.

Spoons (one less than the number of players)

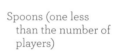

HOW TO PLAY:

The object of the game is to collect four of a kind. Shuffle the deck (don't forget to make sure the jokers are removed). Deal four cards to each player. Place the rest of the deck facedown on the table.

The dealer takes one card from the deck, decides whether or not to keep it, and passes this card, or an unwanted card from the four already in his or her hand, to the person to their left. That person then passes an unwanted card to the player on his or her left, and this keeps going around the group. The last player (the person to the dealer's right) discards a card into a "trash" pile.

"Grab a spoon? Do you know how long it's been since I grabbed a spoon? Do the words 'Billy, don't be a hero' mean anything to you?"

—Ross Geller

The dealer continues to rapidly draw cards from the deck as each player receives a card from the person to their right and passes an unwanted card to the person on their left (with the last player discarding) until a player collects four of a kind. That player grabs a spoon and shouts "Spoon!"

Play as many rounds as you want. When all the rounds are finished, whoever has collected the most spoons is the winner.

Template

WOULD YOU RATHER . . . WITH FRIENDS

Sometimes, it's just hard to decide between two scenarios. This is a great game to play when you're feeling particularly lazy and full but still up for a bizarre mental challenge.

SUPPLIES:
Index cards or scratch paper

Writing utensil for each player

PREP:
Distribute two blank index cards or pieces of scratch paper to each player. Ask players to come up with a silly "would you rather" scenario for each card using references from *Friends*.

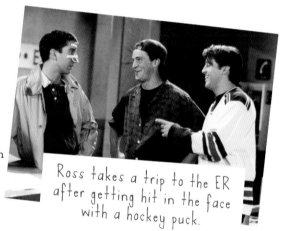

Ross takes a trip to the ER after getting hit in the face with a hockey puck.

HOW TO PLAY:
Put all the completed cards into a pile and shuffle. Each player takes a turn and draws a card, reads it aloud, and answers the question. Meanwhile, other players can try to guess what the player might choose. See who can come up with the strangest "would you rather" scenario.

CHANDLER: Hey, Joe, I gotta ask. The girl from the Xerox place buck naked (holds up one hand) or a big tub of jam (holds up the other hand)?

JOEY: Put your hands together.

HERE ARE TEN CARDS TO START YOU OFF

Would you rather:
Accidentally leave an inappropriate outgoing message on your ex's voicemail . . . or have your first kiss be your brother?

Would you rather:
Have to eat wax when you're starving . . . or have to eat a whole turkey in one sitting?

Would you rather:
Eat a slice of Rachel's trifle . . . or drink the fat?

Would you rather:
Date your sister's stalker . . . or date your own stalker?

Would you rather:
Ask a friend to pee on your jellyfish sting . . . or be asked to pee on a friend's jellyfish sting?

Would you rather:
Get hit in the face with a hockey puck . . . or burn your hand in a round of fireball?

Would you rather:
Have to wear super-tight leather pants all day . . . or seven layers of clothing all day?

Would you rather:
Find a thumb in your soda can . . . or find out that your significant other was responsible for your losing a toe?

Would you rather:
Be known as "the hermaphrodite cheerleader from Long Island" . . . or the person who made out with the fifty-year-old librarian in high school?

Would you rather:
Eat cheesecake off the floor . . . or put your head in a turkey?

YOUR WORST THANKSGIVING MEMORY

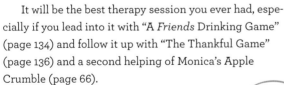

Come on, you know you have a story. Hopefully it doesn't involve losing a toe, being stuck in a box, putting beef in a trifle, eating a whole turkey, or fighting with your sister over who gets your baby if you die, but somewhere deep inside is your worst Thanksgiving memory just waiting to be told to a room full of your closest friends.

SUPPLIES:

Index cards or scratch paper

Writing utensil for each player

HOW TO PLAY:

Have each guest write down his/her worst Thanksgiving memory on a piece of paper. Put the papers in a hat and let everyone pick one. Anyone who picks their own will need to pick again. See if you can guess who each worst memory belongs to. Then commiserate over whose memory was the worst.

It will be the best therapy session you ever had, especially if you lead into it with "A *Friends* Drinking Game" (page 134) and follow it up with "The Thankful Game" (page 136) and a second helping of Monica's Apple Crumble (page 66).

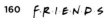

The gang spies on Chandler trying to win his girlfriend back on Thanksgiving after he was stuck in a box for the whole episode.

* * * * * * * * * * *

"Reliving past pain and getting depressed is what Thanksgiving is all about . . . for me anyway, and of course, the Indians."

—Chandler Bing

* * * * * * * * * * *

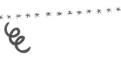

FRIENDS
SECRET IDENTITY

The gang takes on many different identities during the holidays. Ross plays the Holiday Armadillo, Chandler dresses up as Santa Claus, and Joey dons a Superman costume. Now's your chance to have a secret identity too.

SUPPLIES:

Index cards or scratch paper

Writing utensil for each player

Scotch tape

PREP:

Assign each guest one of the characters from *Friends* by taping the name of the character on the back of the player.

HOW TO PLAY:

This game can be played during the course of the party or in one sitting. Players take turns working the room and asking yes or no questions to others to try to figure out their identities. Each player is allowed to ask one question before moving on to the next person. The player who can guess his/her identity with the least number of questions is the winner.

CHARACTER LIST:

- Monica Geller
- Rachel Green
- Phoebe Buffay
- Chandler Bing
- Ross Geller
- Joey Tribbiani
- Janice, Chandler's ex-girlfriend
- Gunther, manager of Central Perk
- Judy Geller, Monica and Ross's mom
- Jack Geller, Monica and Ross's dad
- Frank, Phoebe's brother
- Alice, Phoebe's brother's wife
- Ursula, Phoebe's twin sister
- Mike, Phoebe's husband
- Amy, Rachel's sister
- Jill, Rachel's sister

- Carol, Ross's ex-wife
- Ben, Ross's son
- Emma, Rachel and Ross's baby
- Richard, Monica's ex-boyfriend
- Julie, Ross's ex-girlfriend with whom he returns from China
- Emily, Ross's British ex-wife
- The Holiday Armadillo
- Ugly Naked Guy

Superman and Santa crash the Holiday Armadillo's Chanukah party.

UNAGI
PICTIONARY

Classic Ross. He tries to teach Rachel and Phoebe the power of "total awareness," except it turns out that *unagi* is actually the Japanese word for a "freshwater eel" and not a type of martial arts. See if you and your friends can keep your *Friends* terminology straight with a power game of Unagi Pictionary.

SUPPLIES:

Index cards or scratch paper

Writing utensil for each player

Whiteboard or large paper to draw on

Dry-erase marker or Sharpie

PREP:

Use the suggestions below to create cards listing characters, props, and food from the show, then ask your friends to come up with some too. Once everyone is finished, shuffle the cards. Here are some cards to start you off:

CHARACTERS

• Rachel Green

• Monica Geller

• Phoebe Buffay

• Joey Tribbiani

• Chandler Bing

• Ross Geller

• Any guest stars and recurring characters you want to include (see "Scene: Guess Which *Friends* Character I Am," page 148).

When Ross took "unagi" one step too far.

PROPS

- The white dog statue in the guys' apartment

- The reclining chairs in the guys' apartment

- A coffee cup from Central Perk

- Phoebe's guitar

- The peephole frame on Monica's door

- The foosball table

- The turkey with sunglasses

- The chick

- The duck

FOOD

(Hint: you might see some of these in the recipe section in this book.)

- The Moist Maker
- Trifle
- Cranberries
- Yams
- Chocolate chip cookies
- Meatball sub
- Pizza

- Salad
- Steak
- Cheesecake
- Lasagna
- Brownies
- Grilled cheese

HOW TO PLAY:

Divide into two teams. One player from a team picks a card from the deck and announces the category: character, props, or food. If a guest star or recurring character is picked, you might want to give a heads-up that it's not a main cast member. The opposing team sets a timer (using a smartphone) for one minute. The player then has sixty seconds to draw what's on the card while their team tries to guess what it is. Remember, players are not allowed to use words, numbers, gestures, or any other cues. "Oh . . . My . . . God." Good luck!

"Unagi is a total state of awareness. Only by achieving true unagi can you be prepared for any danger that may befall you."

—Ross Geller

CUT THE MOCKOLATE

This game is just about as silly as the mere idea of Mockolate ("a completely synthetic chocolate substitute"), which makes it absolutely perfect for when you and your friends have serious food coma, can hardly move or eat another bite, and need a good laugh. Warning: Do not consume Mockolate if you have allergies to cats.

SUPPLIES:

1 pair of oven mitts

1 scarf to use as a blindfold

1 piece of paper

Writing utensil

1 chocolate candy bar

1 plate

1 fork and 1 knife

"Given the right marketing, we can make Thanksgiving the Mockolate holiday."
—Mr. Rastatter

PREP:

Wrap a piece of paper around a chocolate candy bar (any kind will do) and write "Mockolate" on it.

HOW TO PLAY:

One at a time, each player puts on the oven mitts and blindfold and tries to cut the Mockolate on the plate using a fork and knife. Yes, this is just as absurd as it sounds. Whoever successfully cuts a real piece of Mockolate first gets to keep the candy bar as a souvenir—not that anyone will want it at this point, but it's a fun memento! Make sure to snap some candids.

FOSSIL DIG

Your friends will be shocked and more than a little giddy to learn that you've discovered dinosaur bones in your own backyard. You need their help to dig them up, so you've made it into a little competition. I mean, what *Friends* fan wouldn't want to dig for fossils?

SUPPLIES:

A large plastic mat (a tablecloth from a dollar store works great)

2 10- or 12-quart utility buckets

A whole bunch of sand (one 50-pound bag of play sand will do)

20 assorted dinosaur skeleton fossil toys (available online as a set)

PREP:

Designate an area for your archaeological site. Most likely you will want to do this outside. Spread out a large plastic mat and place your buckets on top of it with enough distance apart that each team has space to dig. Fill each bucket with sand halfway to three-quarters full, and as you're filling, drop ten dinosaur fossils inside each bucket at varying depths.

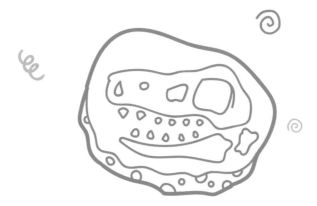

"Come on, Ross, you're a paleontologist. Dig a little deeper."
—Phoebe Buffay

HOW TO PLAY:

Designate two players from each team to be the diggers. Set a timer on a smartphone for sixty seconds. The first team to find all the fossils first (or the most fossils) wins. Feel free to hide more fossils and play again as many times as you want. Then reward yourselves for your hard work with some Neslé Toulouse Brown Butter Chocolate Chip Cookies (page 72).

A FRIENDSGIVING WORD STORY

This activity is a variation on the classic "One Word Story" improv game where everyone goes around a circle and says one word in order to make a story. This version starts each story off with a word that only *Friends* fans will appreciate the *true* significance of.

SUPPLIES:
Note cards or scratch paper torn into small pieces

Writing utensils

PREP:
Create a set of game cards using the word list on the next page.

HOW TO PLAY:
Sit in a circle or group and decide who will go first. One player picks a card and uses that word to start a sentence. Each player to the person's left then takes a turn to add one word of their own until the players have made a complete story. Try your best not to repeat the word from the card. When you're ready to bring the story to a close, say "period." Then, the next player picks a card and starts a new story.

When everyone is late to Phoebe's birthday dinner, Joey has trouble containing his hunger.

WORD LIST:

- Turkey
- Unagi
- Yemen
- Apothecary
- Phalange
- Transponster
- Pivot
- Moist Maker
- Seven
- Princess Consuela Banana Hammock
- Gleba
- Armadillo
- Cheesecake
- Nubbin
- Lobster
- Break
- Moo
- Hi
- Smelly
- Break

"That's a great story. Can I eat it?"
—Joey Tribbiani

DRINK WITH FRIENDS FROM A TO Z!

This game is a great way to practice your alphabet skills with your best buds and favorite beverages (with or without alcohol)!

SUPPLIES:
Beverage of choice for each player

HOW TO PLAY:
Starting with the letter *A* and going in order of the alphabet, each player has to come up with a word or phrase from *Friends* that begins with the letter received on their turn. Words can include names, places, and objects from the show. Phrases count too if they include a word that starts with the given letter. For example, if the letter is *D* and the player's answer is "How you doin'?," that would be acceptable. If a player cannot come up with a word or phrase for the letter, then he/she has to drink and the next player attempts to come up with a word or phrase for that letter.

HERE'S 100 PERCENT PROOF THAT YOU CAN MAKE IT FROM A TO Z:

A: apartment, apothecary, airplane, Amy

B: break, beer, *Baywatch*, bagpipes

C: coffee, Central Perk, Chandler, cups, Consuela Banana Hammock, chick, canoe

D: dinosaur, drink, Dr. Drake Ramoray, divorce, duck, dog

E: embryos, Emily, Eddie

F: *Friends*, foosball, Frank Jr., flan, French

G: Gunther, guitar, Geller, Green

H: hockey, Holiday Armadillo, "How you doin'?"

I: ice, "I know!"

J: jam, jellyfish, Joey, Jill, Janice

K: Kate . . . and also "kick-you-in-the-crotch-spit-on-your-neck fantastic"

L: lasagna, lobster

M: Monica, Marcel, monkey

N: nap, Ugly Naked Guy

O: ovaries, *Old Yeller*

P: pivot, Phoebe, Monica's Tiki Death Punch, pizza, "pla"

Q: quiche

R: Rachel, Ross, Richard

S: sandwiches, salad, superhero, Superman, Smelly Cat

T: trifle, transponster

U: unagi, umbrellas

V: venereal disease, Vegas

W: "We were on a break!," weddings

X: Xerox (as in "the hot girl from the Xerox place" who Ross cheated on Rachel with when they were "on a break")

Y: Yemen

Z: Mr. Zelner (Rachel's boss at Ralph Lauren); Zamboni (Okay, you got me, there was no Zamboni. But there was a hockey game, so go ahead and use it!)

ACKNOWLEDGMENTS

It seems fitting for a book about Friendsgiving that I feel thankful to many people.

Thank you to my phenomenal editors at Running Press. Cindy Sipala, this was our third *Friends* book together and the biggest one I've ever written. Thank you for the opportunity, for all of your heart-felt encouragement and guidance, and for trusting me when I said I had "a streak of Martha Stewart" in me. Jess Riordan, thank you so much for your expert guidance, editing prowess, and speedy turnarounds. You rock! Thank you also to copyeditor Sarah Scheffel, proofreaders Margaret Moore and Nanette Bendyna, production editor Katherine Furman, Celeste Joyce for the lovely cover, and Ashley Prine at Tandem Books for the beautiful design.

Thank you to the dynamic Warner Bros. team, Victoria Selover and Katie Campbell. Victoria, what a treat to have you edit this book after working with you as a colleague for many years.

Loads of thanks and hugs to my family and friends for their love, friendship, and nuggets of food and entertaining wisdom over the years.

To my parents, Beth and Howard Cohen, thank you for always encouraging my love of writing and for all the home-cooked meals growing up. I'm not going to lie—there was a lot of chicken . . . but it was always good. Dad, thanks for instilling within me the greatest gem when it comes to preparing meat: "First, you pound it." You guys are the greatest and I love you.

To my Grandma Claire Gottlieb, when it comes to cooking and entertaining, you are one classy lady, not to mention a brilliant scholar and snazzy dresser. Thank you to you and Grandpa Milton Gottlieb for being such an inspiration to me.

To my Aunt Renee Cohen, I can't thank you enough for giving me the best gift when I got married—a handwritten binder with all of my Grandma Lee Cohen's recipes. Thank you for that and for your help with this book. I see an eggplant appetizer in your future.

To my dear mother-in-law, Judy Stopek, thank you for encouraging me to be more adventurous with cooking. Thanks to you, I fancy myself a connoisseur in the art of using fresh herbs and whatever I have in my vegetable drawer. I continue to learn from you, especially when it comes to hosting and roasting with love!

Andrea Shear, what would I have done without you?! Thank you for baking with me, helping me with recipes, letting me bounce ideas off you, and above all, for your one-of-a-kind friendship. "I'll be there for *you*" whenever you need.

Jean Michel Alperin, thank you for providing expert mixology. Let's grab a drink soon!

Thank you to Mark Bittman, Ina Garten, and Martha Stewart, for being there for me in the kitchen and at the parties, whether you know it or not.

To my beloveds—my husband, Jon, and my daughter, Sasha—thank you for giving me the time to write, the space to cook, and for binge-watching *Friends* episodes with me while I worked on this book. Your love, support, patience, and laughter carried me through, like always. And baby, you are my "lobster."

Last, but certainly not least, thank you to the supremely talented writers, producers, directors, cast, and everyone who had a hand in making *Friends*. It's not every day that I get the opportunity to work on a project like this, and it wouldn't exist without the incredible show you created. I'm forever grateful to you for giving us the gift of *Friends*.

P.S. Jennifer Aniston, DM me—let's do Friendsgiving together!

ABOUT THE AUTHOR

Shoshana Stopek is the author of numerous pop culture–themed books, including *Friends: Lessons on Life, Love, and Friendship* and *Friends: The One About You (A Fill-in Book)*, as well as titles that feature Captain Marvel, Spider-Man, Scooby-Doo, and Tom and Jerry. She lives in Los Angeles with her husband and daughter—who are, by far, her two favorite characters.

Photo Credit: Hrush Photography